DISCOVER YOURSELF

Be Successful

AMIT AGRAWAL

authorHOUSE®

AuthorHouse™
1663 Liberty Drive
Bloomington, IN 47403
www.authorhouse.com
Phone: 1 (800) 839-8640

Published by AuthorHouse   10/14/2016

ISBN: 978-1-5246-4540-3 (sc)
ISBN: 978-1-5246-4539-7 (e)

Introduction

Life is an ongoing process, it is always moving. It moves when we are working, it moves when we are going to office, while making preparation for going to office, while sleeping and when we watch T. V. or doing anything.

We generally do not consider many things that we do daily as a part of our routine which takes time and makes life move.

Anything, which takes time, is making our life move, after all biggest and best unit for calculating the life is age of a person, which is calculated by time only.

I am discussing about the things which we perform but do not consider them as part of our life and they take time and makes life move such as thinking, walking, talking and many more things like this.

Why I am emphasizing on this is that life of an individual is nearly about 80-90 years, in which we have hundreds of months, thousands of weeks and thousands of days and around million hours and every hour we perform many activities. Every activity generates some thoughts in our mind and these are the thoughts, which mainly shape our personality and influence our future working.

Our daily interaction in many work areas with both living and non-living things is basically a driver of our thought generation process, through this we develop our personality and we work accordingly.

Everyone in this world is grown with a different surroundings, different surrounding is having different living and non-living things and if all human beings are grown up having different surroundings then all are also having different personality because everyone after all learn from his surrounding only.

A baby born in English speaking family always speak English when he starts speaking & baby born in Hindi speaking family always speak Hindi. This is because they learn these things from their surroundings.

Let me take an easier example – a child is always sent to a good school to groom. It is surroundings of the school, atmosphere around in which that child grow for 17-18 years of his life and learn all the good things about life and shape himself accordingly but in same school and same class there are other children and every children behavior is different. One is good child because he is with the philosophy of school and one having different thoughts is not considered as equally good because he has some different philosophy. So every person have their own thoughts, like the good child has totally influenced by the school education system so he has shaped his thoughts as per school's teaching principle and other child has shaped his thoughts in other way because he is not influenced by school's principle rather some other forces are influencing him, It may be his friend circle or family or any place where he spend his time.

So it is clear from example that every person is having different surroundings and some are influenced by some type of surroundings and some by others and the type of surroundings they get influenced with, that they process their thoughts. .

Continuing example of school children only, in one class there are many students but all do not want to be engineer, some want to be Doctors, some business professionals and some in Army etc. So everyone is taking decision to lead his future life according to characters or thoughts, which have influenced them.

Why I am discussing this all is, it is your surroundings, which totally dominate your thoughts in day-to-day working, and you take decision as per that. In dominance of those surroundings some take good decisions and some take bad decisions. Persons taking good decision are successful and person taking bad decision are not successful.

At work we face many situations having different surroundings, which processes our thoughts, and accordingly we work. Means it is all three words which are driving us, surroundings situations and our thoughts. Thoughts are of two types one are thoughts which we already have developed throughout our life & one are current processing of thoughts. These are the main three things which shape our personality anywhere everywhere.

Let me tell you one fact of life that you may be anywhere in this world at any time with anyone these three things are always there.

These things define human personality and then human personality is having different traits, which we all have to understand to be the successful person at every work place & in our day to day affairs.

Why we have to understand these traits are because the human is totally driven by his traits and if you have to understand yourself or any other human being you have to understand these traits.

I took examples of school children because it is a place where everyone develop his foundation and then on that foundation we all have to build our future.

If we move further and see offices, shops, market places, transportation means roads, factories, picture halls entertainment centers, parties etc. where we observe lot of human beings and they all carry different personalities and on daily basis we have to interact with them to get our work done after all person cannot live in isolation. When we meet these peoples on daily basis some we find good and some we find hard to be friend. On the other hand the person who is hard to be friend for us is very good friend of someone else. <u>Why this is there?</u>

In parties we always observe big crowd and all the person come well dressed and everybody enjoys but there is only few <u>people who are face in the crowd why?</u>

While working in office every employee try their best to impress organization, but <u>why some are close to boss and get high salary hikes.</u>

There are so many people in the world, but why only few are so successful person in their field.

Why one person handle microphone on stage with utter perfection and others not?

What makes some one more visible in every group to lead the team?

Why there is a person who is always happy?

How in this difficult world people makes such a good careers?

Why we find many people with no fear in their eyes and a burning desire to grow?

Why there is a person who is always satisfied?

Why some person is liked by all the friends and relatives?

These thousand types of questions always come to our mind daily but when we try to find the answer of these question we did not find them.

Again we go back to our basic theory that it is understanding of situation, surroundings and thoughts which make all these people successful on this earth. **The personality traits and the theory of situation surroundings and thoughts is main driver of human beings success. It is highly** required. For this we all have to understand how our personality get effected every time in different situation and surroundings and how are we reacting accordingly.

Let's talk about different personality trait and how they get effected with surrounding situation and thoughts.

Contents

Decision Making

Decision Making is a continuous process in our life and every day we make hundreds of decision knowingly and unknowingly. There are small decisions i.e. for what to eat today, when to go market, to go for a drive and many daily life decision etc. We daily make crucial decisions also at our work place. For every single thing for which we make decision there are only two outcomes of decision either it is a good decision or a bad decision, but let me tell you that everyone takes the best available decision according to him or her, no one takes bad decision for himself, but with time it may prove wrong or right.

So now we have to understand decision making process, while taking a decision there is always a situation on which we have to decide, situation is always having some surroundings, which are influencing it with our thoughts, which we have developed by the virtue of our personality throughout our life.

Let us take a common workplace example of decision-making: -

Situation – In a critical meeting Mohan with his Boss and some senior colleagues are discussing some important subject, all of a sudden Mohan's boss said "ok, this work will be finished by Mohan in 3 days and everybody claps on that, however in actual efforts work assigned to Mohan was of 10 days and it is impossible to finish that work in 3 days. It is Mohan turn to comment on that.

Surroundings – All the top management are sitting around with boss.

Thoughts – Here your thoughts, which you have developed through out your life, will decide your answer.

    Case 1 - Some people will amicably pursue the group by their thoughts, that 10 days' work is not possible to be finish in 3 days and take sufficient time and do work easily and meet targets.

    Case 2 - Some people will accept three days' time and work there best still not achieve it. Make their life miserable.

    Case 3 - Some people will counter argument and make boss angry.

So we can understand from the three out comes that in Case No. 1, Mohan is taking more time, to easily finish his work & make everyone happy also, In Case 2 After trying his best also Mohan cannot finish his work & make his life miserable & In Case 3 you offended all your senior colleges.

So generally in many situations we take decisions as our personality has groomed throughout the years and the decision, which you take, will be best decision for you at the time.

Why we take such a decision because we are influenced by our personality, Surroundings and situation. So it is our decision, which makes you happy and sad.

Decision-making is such a critical activity that our whole life's success and failure depends on decision making.

While taking decisions we should be always be aware of that there are many things which already makes impact on our thoughts, and our thinking is biased towards those thoughts. We also have to take care of surroundings. Surroundings at that particular time of decision making plays very vital role. You have to see that surrounding should not over power you in taking a rational decision and thirdly situation should be totally understood by you. Do not take hasty decisions without understanding the situation completely, because situation is always having its impacts throughout your life.

Mohan is a young boy of 18 years pursuing his XIIth from a good school in Mumbai. Mohan's age and his class is such when he has to take a crucial decision that in which field he has to make his career. Let's see what all factors will influence this decision and finally what decision he ends up.

Situation – We already discussed.

Surrounding – Mohan is born in a doctor family and his father is a doctor. He has good idea of scope of doctor's career. Secondly the teachers are trying to influence him for a career of computer engineer. Thirdly his friend circle is there where most of the people want to be computer engineer.

Thoughts – Mohan is an 18-year boy, having his own thinking, which must be influenced by some or other profession in his life and towards which he is inclined. In this case, There are more chances that Mohan will decide his career as a doctor or a computer engineer but If there are other factors also which may change Mohan thinking as well, that is his awareness of present changes and whether he want to make a decision on understanding the future need of market than he will take a decision by suppressing his old pre conceived thinking and going to the rational mind which is really a good as well as tough decision for him. So you can see that decision, which Mohan will going to take, is most likely be the decision, which surrounding and this thoughts will derive him to take.

How to take a decision

> While taking decisions in your life, you should be sure of that every decision has its impact for some time or for more time in your life, as we already discussed some decision make you happy and some decision make you sad, but only the real outcome of a decision you can see when it get matures.
>
> Like setting a business, There may be expertise of a person in a particular area, where he want to set his business, but taking a decision that to set up the business does not means it will successful also. We only come to know how good or bad the decision of setting up a business is when the business start to giving it yields. If you are able to earn from it, it is a good decision taken at that time, if you are unable to make money of it, then it is a bad decision.

How to take right decision: -

(i) Analyze the situation (this analysis should be like a layman understanding where he asked every question to understand it).

(ii) Surrounding - do not allow surroundings to dominate or influence your thinking power.

(iii) Come out of your perceived thinking and go to a rational mind, if possible see objectively of the situation. Your thoughts are the main driver of decision so there should be a balance when you take a decision.

Leadership

2

What is leadership?

How to develop leadership qualities?

What are its advantages?

Leadership is the quality of presenting yourself in a way where people give respect to your thoughts and you drive the group at any place.

Leadership is highly important personality trait because it give you power to make decisions, rational decisions which other accepts. Through leadership you can be successful in every work place because it gives you a stage where people starts respecting you. If you are true leader you can create wonders out of it. Phenomenon of leadership is very simple. I divide leadership in two different way one is a self-leader and other is to be a leader in a group and drive the group in work place.

To be a good leader in work place I strongly recommend you to be a self-leader first and then take charge of a group leader.

To be a self-leader you have to understand yourself first, i.e. what are the requirements of a human being from you?

(i)   Care
(ii)   Love
(iii)   Politeness from other / polite to everybody
(iv)   Happy
(v)   Knowledgeable
(vi)   Vision

(vii)   Versatile
(viii) Confident
(ix)   Maturity
(x)   Decision making
(xi)   Flexibility
(xii)   Discipline
(xiii) Logic

So many more personality traits we will discuss further after understanding the self Requirements. You can always understand other human beings by knowing their requirements and you have to be slightly flexible according to the situation, surroundings and thoughts and let see how it works.

Let me take some practical examples of life. Generally people think that a leader is a person who speaks a lot. This can be a quality of leadership but this is not a leadership.

You all must have noticed many times in a group of 10 people debating on some topic and coming to a conclusion. There are many persons talking and out of 10 people 1 or 2 has taken a lead, all of a sudden a quiet person comes with a marvelous idea to which the group has to accept due to the vision and objectivity of the idea. So this person by quoting one line drive the group and take the charge as a leader due to his knowledge vision and objectivity. How this will come we already have discussed in decision-making.

So the person who talk less can also be leader, for leadership you simply has to analyze the situation make yourself flexible like that, speak with your knowledge and politeness having objectivity in your words and take the charge.

Concept on leadership works on how widely you are accepted within a group. How can person be accepted by understanding others needs and how can he understand others need by understanding his own needs.

When we talk about leadership qualities two things play very important role i.e. your adaptability and flexibility.

Still our basic theory remain the same that leaders have to analyze the situation and should be flexible enough to adjust himself with the surroundings and change his thoughts accordingly to come to a great idea.

Let me share some more examples on leadership – In our daily life and at work place many times we work in a team, when we are working in a team it is obvious that many different thoughts and approaches will come from different person for different situations. Now let's analyze different situation to be a true leader in-group.

Situation 1– If you are having Good knowledge about the subject, sincerely put your thoughts and get it accepted from the group by putting them in a humble way and sail out as a true leader. When you really have knowledge about that subject three things play very crucial role – You should be sincere, disciplined and confident when taking the charge. Never put them in granted manner otherwise after having true knowledge also, it will not be accepted in-group.

Situation 2 – If you have equal knowledge of the subject as other members are having then speak when your turn will come and try to give respect to other thoughts also. Listen properly to others thoughts, which can resolve the situation and give everyone, equal opportunity to talk. Do not try to impose your thoughts on someone if you are not sure they are correct, do not try to lead the group by thoughts, try to accumulate thoughts from the group only and conclude.

Situation 3 – If you have no knowledge of the subject then only listen to group as a good listeners where you have to respect other thoughts and listen to them so quietly that they will love talking to you. Listen to everyone with delight and make everyone impressed by your listening attitude and try to ask some question midway, so that you can lead by raising doubts and plunging the loop holes.

So it is required for a leader that he also have to respect other's thoughts if he is not having knowledge on that particular subject.

Person can be a leader or a successful man in many ways, there are many personality traits, which make a man, true leader, which will discuss in later parts.

Confidence 3

What

Confidence is inner courage of a person to face any situation, surroundings and thoughts with attitude of solving it. Confidence is also a main driver to success.

Advantage

There are many situations, which only confident person can face, because these situations have such surroundings that without having confidence your thoughts will change and you will, unable to face that situation.

How

Confidence is a personality trait, which always comes to a person when he starts facing the difficult situations. So first thing which we have to keep in mind is that, to develop confident personality, we have to start facing difficult situations.

Difficult situation means any calculated risk, which is different from a normal behavior. For confidence you did not require anything extra, it comes to you if you have good knowledge about the subject.

Let us understand confidence in other way also – when a person is doing a routine work he is in a situation and surroundings, which he is used to and he feels very comfortable. Any situation which makes you feeling uncomfortable generates many thoughts in your mind which leads you to negative direction i.e. depression, anger, frustration etc. So here you to have to take decisions with your inner confidence that you have developed.

How to develop it?

We will start with an example: -

Mohan was coming to office by his car and in between his trouser got torn slightly when he was coming out of car at office parking. Mohan was very particular about his dressing, so he thought that how with a hole in his trousers he can go into the office, he thought of returning back home and change the trousers but there was a very important meeting scheduled after 5 minutes.

So he has having no option but to walk to the office and attend the meeting and then afterwards get the trouser changed.

Mohan entered the meeting room with utter care that no one can see that his trouser is having any hole and he sat on meeting chair.

Meeting lasted for 1 hour and every person went to his work place i.e. no one noticed that Mohan's trouser is having any hole, on this Mohan decided to spend whole day in office with that trouser only and he spend it and no one in office noticed it. (Out of 100 people on a road only one person noticed that you are wearing a teared trouser and that person does not mean much to us.)

People are having stage fear, but there is no word like stage fear because on stage everyone has to go for the first time and you are also one of them – secondly on stage also you tumble your intensity of thing over is 100% but audience does not care for it only 5% people notice that.

We can analyze that, without any reason people lose their confidence to do things.

Here we can say now that do your work, if you are confident about it, you will able to finish it, if you make 5% error also you are allowed because you are human, learn from those mistakes and do not perform mistakes from next time because your first mistakes will not going to be noticed if you are able to finish it perfectly subsequently. .

So how to develop confidence is to work in any situation and surrounding as per requirement without thinking what others will think about it.

Every successful and confident man on this earth is today confident because he has already master of his subject, so he is always comfortable in different situations, which comes to him, and he performs better.

Let's take example – If you are a good manager you feel good working in an office with your staff because that is comfortable place for you, you are used to that situations and surroundings.

So everything that you do for the first time you are not sure of success and many negative thoughts surround you and you lose confidence to do it.

Let me tell you for developing confidence you have to have an attitude of facing any situation at any surrounding for the first time with what all personality you are having. Every successful man has to face many things first time but they develop attitude of determination from their personality that they handle it with perfection.

When every person has to handle one or other situation first time then how can we be different, we are also handling many things for the first time, so be determinant and handle it with what all personality you are having.

You take initiative in your life and your personality will be equipped by the personality trait of confidence and then you can perform many things which you were afraid of doing previously.

Let me tell you one thing that if you want to be big and true leader at every workplace you have to develop an approach of taking initiatives from you personality trait of confidence.

Vision

4

The power of analyzing things much before when they actually happened is called as vision.

Vision is very required quality of a leader and successful manger.

Vision is a personality trait that is developed in an individual by the way he takes situation, analyze surroundings and shape his thoughts.

In today's world vision is very much required. Today everything is fast changing, you have to perform or take any decision by analyzing what impact that decision should be having in future. It all comes from what vision a person is having.

Vision also means how much ahead a person can think of his fellow mates.

If we see today's life, it is so much busy that no person is able to come out of his routine activities to think ahead. 30 years back who has dare to think that computer processor like i7 are possible, but Intel has vision and he made it also.

How it comes:-

In daily life, managers have to take many decisions, for every decision you have some situation, surroundings and your thoughts through which you decide what the best decision at that time is.

Vision gets develop when you take every situation, surrounding as a new challenge and decide the outcome by not getting influenced by your old thoughts.

In Earlier world when we were not having good education system and awareness is very less due to lack of communication system etc. If you see trend of people working it is very predictable that if it is a farmer's family, his son will also do farming, if it is cobblers family, his son will also become a cobbler and if it's a general merchant's son, then he will also become general merchant. So people follow only what their ancestor have done in past, because no one has open mind and they only act according to their preconceived thoughts.

This means for creating a vision in personality you have to welcome every thought, you should not have any mental block, because vision means only that you are thinking ahead with some new changes in your mind.

As new communication system comes in place, people's awareness starts developing fast, so you can see that development in last 1000 years in comparison to last 100 years, there is a big difference. We all have developed ourselves in last 100 years with the very fast pace due to the awareness. So the awareness is the tool that give you thinking openly with rational mind.

So vision is developed by a free mind having lot of awareness about the surroundings.

Through vision, managers have to take many decisions, some are the decisions which effect only your routine work, but there are some decision which will going to affect everyone on the earth after 5-10 years hence, every small or big business is started by the person having vision only, he is putting money today to get returns tomorrow. The only difference between the business are size of business, some people are having bigger vision they go for big thinking and some are having small vision they go for small thinking.

Vision comes from decision-making, leadership and confident qualities.

One more important thing, which counts in taking decision ahead, is your risk taking capacity. Vision that you are having is an unseen future approach based on your knowledge and awareness about this world. To implement and work on that you require some courage to go on that path, so if you have any vision and you are slightly doubtful about its success, so don't bother about that, it is human mind. It always resist new changes and give lot of doubts about success when you are working for your vision for success but at this time only you have to develop risk taking capacity and(we talk risk in risk chapter) work accordingly.

Stress 5

When a person is in a situation and surrounding which are not comfortable for him, his mind processes thoughts, which are in negative direction, and this makes him uncomfortable. Situation of a person is driver of stress in a human being.

Stress is such a common personality trait that we can find in every person across the globe. But the level of magnitude of stress is different from person to person.

There are lot of disadvantages of stress on your health as well as on your growth and prosperity. A stressful person is giving invitation to different medical hazards as well your professional life also gets ruined.

Stress leads to negative personality traits in a person, i.e. anger, frustration, sadness, fear, etc.

If you develop stress fast then you will suffer at your house as well as at office. Due to stress,

(i) You have not cordial relation with your Boss.

(ii) Your colleagues also start disliking you.

(iii) Your work suffer.

(iv) Your family is also not happy

(v) Soon you are in a hand of various medical disorders.

How it comes?

Stress comes to person from different activities that he perform in his daily life.

Let's take a very simple example of stress – After coming to home from our workplace, if we make this habit to keep all the required document and articles at a pre-defined place so that next day when we go office we can pick all those things from there, but we generally do not do this.

Next morning when we start preparation for going to office, all the things that we want to carry, we never find them. When we not find the things we search them because they are required to be with us when we are in office. Searching things takes time and when it takes time we started worrying about reaching the office late.

So one small thing puzzled a person so much that stress get developed.

Again we go back to our basic theory of situation, surroundings and thoughts. Every person has personality to face the different situation and surroundings. Some person who develops the thought by comparing themselves with others and gets jealous from others also develops lot of stress.

Means your thoughts and attitude towards life also generates stress i.e. if you compare yourself with others than you always find other side of grass more greener.

How to avoid stress?

For avoiding stress we have to keep in our mind that all the small things, which are happening in our daily life, are having future effects. So while doing anything in your life do it in a planned manner so that in future if you require it, it is always accessible to you.

Comparisons about anything in the life should be avoided, because there is no parameter for comparison. You always compare yourself with the best, but you did not see the reason behind a person or anything on the earth to be best.

Example: - There is very common phenomenon of two human being comparing each other, I strongly want you all to avoid this comparison, most of the human stress develops due to comparisons only.

I don't know why we compare each other, tell me one thing how can other person's growth or happiness harm you, if you are doing your work with sincerity.

Rather if other person is your good friend, his growth will help you in growing.

Believe me in today's world no one has time to intervene in our activities and do bad for us, but we only create such a thoughts inside us that will make us to think that his growth will make us unhappy.

I have very effective way of working in these type of cases and I also suggest you to go for it, otherwise it causes stress and it hamper us physically as well as professionally.

At the time when this comparing attitude comes to you, try to analyze your life and then if you know about the person try to analyze his life also.

You will find you have not achieved less then him, rather you have achieved the best what you can achieve from the surrounding and situation you have till date in your life.

Person born and brought up at metros cities are sometimes have more exposure than the person born and brought up at village – why to compare such persons, it is not greatness of that person that he is having such a great personality, it is his surroundings which has made him great. If village born person also has grown in similar surroundings, then he has also grown same way.

Please take a note of this that every person when born is having two hands, two legs and a brain. This brain is like a blank cassette. It is on his surroundings, which decides to fill in that. So as a human being you not have to blame yourself for not to be best, rather if now you have surroundings like that which are good so adapt that and learn best out of it. So that when others will see you after some time he will want to be like you and when this phenomenon continues than everyone in this world will be a fully developed person with all the happiness and no stress.

Basically if we see that stress is our self-generated negative thoughts. So in our life, if we keep broad mind and good attitude stress can easily be controlled.

Stress is not like a wound which will cause you pain anyway but it is like a car driving that if you drive car safely there is no chance of accident, same if you controlled your action as per the situations and surroundings you can have no stress at all.

People have a general tendency of thinking over small things. If anything goes wrong in some one life then he thinks for many weeks and months, but tell me, if someone lost his wealth in some incident then it will not come by thinking about that thing for long, it will only come back when you are determined to get it back and work for it. Thinking for something lost will only give you stress not that thing comes back. This is generally applicable for everything.

If you want to be a leader, successful manager and happy human being you should have to understand that your own self creates stress as you create other personality traits by understanding low things, which explain you, can control stress.

Perception

6

Perception is:- How you look at the things from your point of view, To make you understand about the perception we have to see one example of an elephant.

There was a management game played in an office where you have to touch the things by closing the eyes and visualize about that particular thing.

One elephant sculpture was kept for everyone to touch and guess what it is. So one by one every person started touching the sculpture. Person who touched the legs of the elephant thought it is a pillar, person who touched the tail thought it is a kind of snake and some who touched the trunk thought it is a duct pipe, but they all were wrong, it was an elephant.

If you see this example from every individual point of view they were right because what they touch they visualize but actually it was something else. This is a very common phenomenon in life, every person visualize things from their point of view but holistic view sometimes comes out to be different and their decisions are proved to be wrong.

So perception is a process of visualizing the situations from your point of view, it may be as per the surroundings or it may also be only your point of view. In these situations what you perceive, through that you develop your thoughts and accordingly you react.

Why perception understanding required?

Perception is not a personality trait but perception is a driver, which help you to generate personality traits. Let me tell you both positive as well as negative perception impact on a human being personality.

After finishing my education, I came to Mumbai with lot of ambition in my perceived mind that Mumbai is a city of dreams and everyone who comes to Mumbai achieve success. As I have perceived something good about Mumbai, my personality traits start working in that direction, means my confidence, leadership, decision making etc. traits are started favoring me, because I have in my mind that I landed in a city of success. So it is your perceived mind, which has taken your total charge, and it is driving you. Likewise you go to any astrologer if he predicts that coming week is good for you then again all the personality traits starts working in such a positive direction that will actually take your week good. So it is very simple that your perception takes charge of your situation and drives you accordingly.

Now let's see how, it work in negative direction -: I took a rented house in Mumbai after looking at 12-15 houses. I was very happy with my decision that I have taken a good house. I told my friends that I am happy taking a good house on rent. I told them the address of house and location also.

After listening the address some friends told that the place where I took the house is having some bad smell from nearby factories and there is some water problem also.

See how perception works – My friend who is a local Mumbai person when told about smell and water problem I have to believe him.

My happiness, confidence change to frustration and fear of taking wrong decision. Now I started cursing self that why I took this decision in hurry and make my one-week miserable, till arrival of my weeks which was schedule a week later. I was very apprehensive to tell her about the smell and water problem.

I made my week miserable by having these thoughts, I already have given the brokerage and rent to the landlord, so now I also cannot change my decision.

After one week, my wife arrived and we unloaded all our household goods and arranged them in house, I did not told anything to my wife regarding the smell and water problem.

We started living there and days, weeks and months passed on and my wife did not complained me about anything nor I noticed any problem, so I thought of asking about this from my neighbor who is good friend of mine after a month. I asked him is there any problem earlier of water and smell.

My neighbor told me that from last two years he is living in this house and earlier there was some chemical factory and some fumes of chemical factory used to comes here which were creating smell but now that factory is already been closed so no question of any smell, regarding water shortage we only have faced this for one day when we have decided to clean the overhead water tank four months back, now there is no problem.

After listening these facts my thoughts again changed to positive and again I started feeling bit more happy, confident and satisfied.

Earlier when my friend told me about the problem in the flat he told me from his partial knowledge same way I also took it from him and make my life miserable.

So whenever you decide to do something in your life do not make a mountain out of a mole.

Life is not that much complicated what we make it, rather it is very simple. We just organize our thoughts like such that they start giving us pain.

So many thoughts we generate in our mind without taking a complete picture of a particular situation.

For a successful manager and an effective leader you have to understand a particular problem completely for solution, do not reach to a conclusion without analyzing it fully.

Sometimes we unnecessarily create perception of negative thoughts where there is no requirement for them, because it is not a complicated situation.

So control your perception as much as you can.

Look human being has to face many situations in his life where he has to take decision. Do not take any decision by understanding partial situation because it will affect your thinking and thoughts

Teamwork

7

Working together to achieve same goal is teamwork. Teamwork is very required quality for your personality, leadership and to be successful manager.

Generally people confuse teamwork with a team of 5-6 people in an office controlled by a boss. A team is created at workplace for meeting companies objectives. In one sense teamwork definition described above is also correct but it is giving us a very small meaning of teamwork.

Teamwork has got a very big definition, most of the time in our daily life & at our work place knowingly or unknowingly we work in team only. So it is a required personality trait for an individual to be a good team member otherwise we will face stress and it will also hamper our development towards a successful manager and as a leader.

Teamwork starts from your family, your father, mother, brothers, sisters and you, this is a close team only i.e. and in house also we work in a team. So the first lesson we learn from our house only of team work i.e. sharing of work, respect of others thoughts, love with each other and goal of living happily.

So the beautiful team of house teaches us many things, same we build a team when we are husband wife and children. Family is really such a close team where people starts understanding other people also.

In family team also you must have definitely observed that many times some differences occur due to lack of teamwork among the members.

So teamwork is sharing, loving, respecting, understanding and distribution of work and feelings of others in that particular group.

You go to office or college by your car, bike or bus, there also a unknowingly teamwork is taking place, means on road every one moves as per traffic rules only, otherwise there would be traffic jam and if anyone breaks teamwork rules it is a disturbance in work.

If you are travelling through bus or a train it is a coordination between the bus driver, conductor, traffic rules and you, same with train also.

When you reach office you work in a team to achieve your organization's objectives and when you go for lunch in office your canteen people work in a team to serve you with lunch. So teamwork is coming everywhere at every level. You cannot be ignorant with everyone and live life aloof. You have to interact with some or the other persons for achievements of your goals, desire and vision to be fulfilled. Means you also form a team depending on requirement, it may happen that sometimes you are part of team which is working and producing results and sometimes you are person who is benefited by others coordinated work, depending upon the situations and surroundings.

So if teamwork is so much important, are you a good team player, and if you are not a good team player then maybe you are not getting all those thing, which you deserve. Let us analyze how to be a good team player – I give you a very common example, which you must also have observed in your life but have not analyzed it:-

Leaders are the very good example of teamwork player, no person from his birth is a leader. He understand others in a manner that he get respect for his thoughts at every situation and at every work place.

Same like at work place also it is not necessary that most intelligent person is a best team player.

In a team you should always have to behave in a way you like behavior for yourselves from others, don't think that you ignore a person and he will love you, respect come from respect only, you respect others they respect you.

Team work also comes with your compatibility with others, if in a group there are two persons who never listen to others and only impose their decision, they can be compatible to group if they are really having knowledge about the subject or a boss can be compatible in this way otherwise team cannot be form rather there will be stress among the members.

So teamwork includes listening others also, if good orator is a quality than good listener is also a quality.

Do not hurt person's feelings when you are part of a team, your presence should be always a support for your team members, if you have approach of supporting others then there is no reason that others will not support you. If someone still behave erratic means something goes wrong with him try to analyze person if you are able to understand him it is good otherwise ignore him till he give you stress.

Be always humble and polite when you are talking to a person in a team, if you are debating on some burning issue aggressive approach can work.

Rigidness, anger, ego and jealousy are the words, which you totally have to eradicate from your personality because these personality traits will first make you odd man out in the group and then burn your own self also. (We will discuss them in later sessions of book).

Think Big 8

Thinking big means to have capabilities of visualizing your future work aspects with a vision where you can perform better than normal.

Thinking big is an aspect of personality where you all have to come out of your normal working and slightly give more efforts to your working style with new creative thinking, it comes out with a better results which will put you different from others.

Let's try to understand it more, we all have heard this saying that shoot at a star you will landed up with moon. Means till the time you will not generate capabilities to think big then how can you achieve big rather normal also.

Think big is very simple concept of life that set your goal always higher than what you have to achieve in your life. If you can achieve these higher goals it is well and good but the intense preparation of achieving those higher goals will make you to achieve your normal goals easily. When we think for a bigger goal to achieve then all our personality traits work in positive direction and give us a boost to achieve that because we generate a feeling inside that this is a big achievement. This will make us to work day and night, same way if you feel that the goal will be set for you is easy and achieving goal will not give you any achievement than your personality traits will not boost your personality.

How to go for it: - Daily in office you have to meet many customers to solve their grievance about your company. Your company has fixed a target of meeting 60 people in a day. You fix your own target of meeting with 90 people a day and solve their grievance with quality. It will be a difficult job for you initially but when you try it with all your determination you can achieve it also. Once you achieve it then you are person who is not a normal person, you have proved yourself to be an achiever and at workplace also you will feel very comfortable in meeting normal target of 60.

Thinking big is a more of an attitude, approach and vision of a person which he develop from his personality, for thinking big you have to broaden your vision and have to think beyond boundaries. You are not allowed to sit in the cocoon and do your normal work but you have to break it out and perform work which are having no boundaries.

For this you have to understand your personality and shape it for bigger achievements.

Let me try to make you understand once more – In today's world most of the person who have created big names and big wealth are not wealthy 100 years ago. These people have created their business empires by thinking big, i.e. if they have also followed the same route of their ancestors by doing their normal work then today they would not have been so much famous.

For becoming rich, wealthy they come out of their old working style and worked in a more creative manner without boundaries. So no one is born rich or big, every person has thought differently, creatively and without boundaries to reach at this level. So it is highly required aspect of your personality to have capabilities to think limitless without boundaries to achieve very big.

Now take a case where your surroundings and situations are not making your thoughts to think big, growth will be slow and hamper, typical example of Indian villages. People daily work in same surroundings and situations due to lack of awareness, then how can they grow.

In cities people are growing because they think by coming out of their cocoon and this comes from the awareness and awareness comes from the different information systems.

So to think big you have to create surrounding where you have a complete awareness of your field, through different situation you have to develop your vision, decision-making approach, risk taking capacity, confidence.

Then your thoughts will be shaped in a way that you will think differently and big that you will really change your whole life.

Attitude

9

Attitude is an approach of human mind for solving different challenges he faces in his daily life.

Attitude is developed by a human from his different personality traits as well as attitude is required to develop personality traits in a human being.

Attitudes are basically of two types one is positive attitude towards life and second is negative attitude.

Let's take some example to understand attitude: - When we make some good achievements in our office place, some of our colleagues and boss comes and praises us and congratulate us on the achievements through their positive attitude, share the happiness.

Same time some colleagues feel bad on our achievements, but this is due to their attitude towards us may be they are not comfortable with us, that's why they have created negative attitude.

So first thing which we have to understand about attitude is that, in different situation person behaves with different attitudes. If someone is rude in nature with you doesn't mean that he is rude with everybody he may be comfortable somewhere else where his attitude may change.

Importance of Attitude :- Attitude of a person totally control him, if you have positive attitude towards some things and negative attitude towards other things, you can survive by the balance of both but try whole of life that you always have positive attitude towards most of the things because your personality is reflected by your attitude.

Secondly, person who developed positive attitude towards life are generally successful but persons who develop negative attitude towards life makes their life miserable. All the decision that we take in daily life are all dependent on our attitude.

Example:-

Sometimes you must have noticed that people come out from very difficult situation becomes successful because of their positive attitude only, Doctors also advice patients that to be healthy and fit you first have to generate positive attitude towards life and then only medicines will work. People who get disable due to some accidents and are unable to walk, starts working if they generate positive attitude towards life.

Positive attitude: - This is approach of mind where you are confident of solving any challenge whatever comes to your life at whatever time.

Negative attitude: - In this case you have approach of mind where fear, frustration and feeling of insecurity lies and you are doubtful about your capabilities.

How these positive and negative attitudes get generated and how to control them?

Positive Attitude: - This attitude get developed from the way you take things in your life. For developing positive attitude you have to keep in your mind that requirement is a mother of all invention. So all the problem which you will be going to face in your life will be solved because they all are having solutions, only we have to think them twice before taking any decision. Secondly if at all, some problem is not having any solution than invention will going to take place and that will be solved. You people must be thinking of that, how I am highly optimistic about life, but believe me this works. If you make a positive attitude in life about everything, you can create miracles.

Earlier in your life you have come across many challenges which were new and difficult for you at that time, but you have still faced them and come out with good results means you already have developed many positive features of attitude i.e. taking challenges working hard, leadership, innovation etc. Means now problem are coming to you and you must be facing them as normal routine because you already have conquered the approach of solving problem long back.

So now when any difficult situation comes to your path, your frustration, anger, jealousy and all the thoughts, which can imbalance you, are in control because you have generated an approach of solving problems and this approach generates your attitude.

So your mind and thoughts are well at place and situation either normal or difficult will be unable to imbalance you and you will not reach in a way where people will feel bad and we lost our career prospects.

When we have generated thoughts in our mind of insecurity and doubtfulness from different situation of life, then the birth of negative attitude comes to our life and it give us a setback in our professional life. We lose trust on others, we are not able to handle things confidently and feeling of insecurity and jealousy arises which will hamper our professional life.

How to enhance positive attitude and control negative attitude?

If during your life you have developed negative attitude towards life and you are not sure of your success in your life and you are unable to understand life and you go on a wrong path because success and failure are your own destination, which you drive through your attitudes.

Let's analyze those three four situations where you were unable to get success due to one or other reason and some other people got succeeded and you lost your faith towards life and developed a negative approach.

Now I ask you to do me a favor and go to meet all those persons who were successful at that time when you failed and ask about their success. If they genuinely tell you the truth then they must have failed more than you and from that failure they have learnt much, that today they are successful or they must be better prepared than you to achieve success.

So in this case why you are developing negative attitude rather you have to be happy to learn this main principle of life that to be more successful you have to be failure first or better prepared.

From next time you prepare better to be successful and surely you will succeed one day.

In many situations and surroundings man is not having any other option to lose and through that he generates negative attitudes. By his thoughts everyone is loser in one or the other situation of life because no one can control all the surroundings.

Let's take an example of drilling a nail on wall. If you are unable to fix it on wall you go and call carpenter he will put it for you and you are happy, because you have solved it. Every problem's concept is same of a situation and surrounding, but the dimension changes and sometimes dimension of problem is so big, that you are unable to control them and develop negative attitude. Fixing a nail you can control the situation by calling a carpenter but if you make a loss in business you cannot ask bank to give you loan again. So you are unable to control the situation and you develop negative approach for life, but you are unable to understand that nothing goes wrong from your side in your loss. It was surrounding which are not in control. So if you started thinking bad about that it will only hurt you and it will not enhance your business profits.

So there is no problem which can make you to change your attitude negative because every problem is driven by its on surrounding and your way of approach can make it easier to solve or worsen it. So if you have the approach towards it, you can solve it easily otherwise you will grip by the problem and be unable to solve it all.

ATTITUDE EXAMPLE

I was on my vacation trip with my wife and we were putting up in a hotel. Next day morning when I wake up, I ask the waiter from where we can get newspaper, he told me that there is a square which is 100 meters away, I can easily go walking and buy a newspaper. So I simply walked from my hotel to buy newspaper but to my surprise I did not find any shop there, so I asked the person there that is there any shop to buy a newspaper? He indicated towards the square where newspapers were fixed with the fencing. What you have to do was to take out any of the paper and the money in the box, which was besides the papers. I took one paper and put a coin in open box there. But I was surprised with this type of working and asked a person passing by my side by that how it works he replied "we have started this system to save money", I did not able to understand so I asked him again to explain. He said that hawker in the morning comes and put all his newspapers and coin box on this square, everyone comes and pick the newspaper and put the coin in the box. By doing this we are getting variety of newspaper and saving hawker's cost of individual house delivery.

Again you can see that no one is touching that open coin box because all are aware of future consequences of that.

So it is again proved that if you have right attitude towards life that it will help you in self building as well as in nation building.

Example –2

I was travelling once from City A to City B (keeping city name anonymous) in a taxi with some of my friends, midway we find a toll tax barrier where no one was standing to monitor the payment made by the persons passing by. It was duty of every person passing from there to insert the coin in the box, which was there, and barrier automatically get opens for 5-10 seconds when you can pass your car. When we were standing at that barrier we saw that everyone is putting the coin and barriers opens and they pass through it. With every insertion of coin barriers opens and the time period for which it remains open was enough to 3-4 cars to pass by. So when car ahead of us inserts the coin in the box and passed by we have enough time to cross barrier without inserting anything but still our taxi driver inserted coin and we passed through the barrier. My friends and I were wondering why not our taxi driver cleared that barrier without paying because there was enough time to pass by.

After remaining silent for 5-10 minutes we asked this question to our driver that why didn't he pass by, when he was having enough time? He remained silent and didn't answer. Our curiosity increased and we asked him again the same question. He replied "I paid because it was written there that we have to pay" but again when we asked that you were having enough time to pass by still you paid why? This time he got furious and said "You people are trying to teach me stealing". We were shocked by his answer, then he explained that if today I do not pay and likewise others also stop paying them how government will earn money for maintenance of the road, without maintenance the road will be damaged within 2-3 months.. Then for maintaining road Government would require fund and thus toll would increase from 5 to 10 and government will also appointed officer to monitor the collection. So by not paying now, I am harming my future.

When we listened the taxi driver views we all get much zapped and from there we learnt that attitude in life is very important personality trait. Attitude not only contributes to you but if everyone is having right attitude then they can also help nation to build stronger.

Learn to Ignore 10

In our daily life we come across certain activities that are not relevant to us, but if we ponder on them then we waste our time and certainly going to develop stress. So if stress get developed then thoughts gets effected and when thoughts get effected attitude towards life changes and when attitude changes towards life we do not wish to do work hard, not give time to good thing, make bad decision etc. i.e. with negative attitude we cannot be a good manager or leader.

Let's understand how many things affects us every day and they are not related to us.

Every person is having friends and some people get influenced by their friends and some people influence their friends it's vice versa process, means your friends are also driving your thoughts (I am taking example of friends however it can be anything which influence your thoughts)

Many things, which your friends are doing and you are also doing them indirectly. Like, if your friend is an active smoker you are a passive smoker, if your friends have optimistic approach you will develop optimistic approach and if your friends are having pessimistic approach, there are chances that you also develop pessimistic approach or change his pessimistic approach to optimistic approach.

So as per your surroundings and situations you are going to develop your thoughts.

But we are talking about many things that we do and that only give us stress that is not required.

How to control these thoughts: -

To control these thoughts is to ignore them. Let's take an example of players, when players play, there is big crowd which cheer them up, there are your supporters and other team's supporters also, so at the time of playing generally supporters of other teams make remarks and try to disappoint players by hooting but players simply ignore it because it is the best solution for them. If players feel bad about those words then it is difficult to play and they can develop stress only, so what they basically believe in is that they ignore all the hooting and take all the cheer up from their supporters and play.

In playground it is understood that players have to face supporters as well as critics so they are already ready for it, that is the reason they manage it also, what about actual life.

My dear friend's actual life is same as a play field, where you have to welcome all the support, which you are getting for your development and growth and ignore all the teasing which comes in your way.

You driving your comfortable car with fun mood on Sunday. All of a sudden other car packed with some irresponsible citizen, join with you on road and overtake your car, also not following the traffic rules, so you face some difficulty but after a minute that car turns to the other road and you are again driving your car with other people who are driving car safely. Similarly 1 hour later someone from the mob pass the comment "Drive slowly you do not know how to drive the car"

These types of comments are common on roads from person we don't know at all, so what to do.

In both the situations you have to ignore and enjoy your Sunday. Let's analyze both the situations.

In first case when car was going from your side and changed it route after 5 minutes, it is true that it has disturbed you for 5 minutes and may be after half an hour you will forget everything also but if you go in argument with those persons driving the other car and try to teach them lesson, that they are not driving safely and this may aggravate situation further, instead you can report to right authorities about that behavior(If you wish so). It is moral responsibility of everyone to tell or correct anything which is going wrong in front of us, but my dear friend tell me simple thing that how many times while commenting anybody on his mistakes we do analysis on ourselves that how much we are also involved in that mistake. Commenting anybody is easy but looking inside our self to find faults and change our behavior is really difficult. So in that car driving example we are only seeing that those irresponsible citizen are not driving safely, maybe we are also not driving our car safely. And if we stop them and argue with them it may change to a fight and we would have spoiled our whole day by the bitter thoughts of that experience, so the best way is to ignore it.

In second incident, where mob has passed comment on you, you might have felt bad about the comment, and thought that why unnecessarily he is passing comment on me, I have to fight with him. Good this shows you are aggressive, hot tempered and brave but does this have any actual meaning in life.

Did these type of element really matters in life that we have to come out of our car and fight with them. You fight with first, second is passing comments unnecessarily. They are part of this behavior because they are still not involved in their development and growth building process. So they have time to do so but we are mature enough to ignore such persons.

Tell me how you rate these two families – Two family go for the picnic same day, one family struck on the road for fighting with the person who passed on the comments and waste there whole day, while other family ignore the comments and went to picnic happily and return back happily.

So, it is obvious that second family is always rated as better because of maturity. This always happen in our life where we struck to situation which really do not require any importance and did not able to give time to really important situations and fall behind in many important areas.

So we have to be mature enough to decide where act is required and where it is not required.

Person who develop personality of ignoring many unimportant things are really successful man because they are concentrating only on relevant and important subjects, so they have more time and less problems then person who are sticking on any irrelevant situation, as they are having more questions and less time to attend some important opportunities in life.

And when we are giving unnecessarily more time and attention to trivial thing chances of getting hurt from others and development of pessimist approach is more possible because on road people pass any vulgar comments as they do not regard who you are, but on important issues we always get respect in solving them.

Friends, I strongly suggest you all have to ignore all those things that are causing destruction in our mind like teasing is very common example. When we join any new work place ignore it because those person, who are not relevant only teases us. While you are working, if there are same people in work group also who teases you then first you correct yourself as per the requirement, then see how fast they starts loving you i.e. the simple example of leadership. So we always have to ignore all those irrelevant things, which are giving only stress to us.

Comparisons, jealousy, feeling of insecurity all are such personality traits which only give us stress because we develop unnecessary notion for them in our mind, actually they does not exist in their physical world.

So we should totally geared us to ignore all the unimportant things, which are only giving us stress, and having no practical use in our growth and development.

Dedication

11

Dedication means to work with all the efforts till you achieve your goal.

Dedication is required in your personal life as well as in your professional life while doing work.

Due to lack of dedication many people leave the work when they are already at a finished verge.

Dedication is always required when you are trying to achieve some goals in your life, person who is dedicated towards achieving them only achieves these goals.

Many persons opt for top Universities examinations and few get selected, the persons who get selected are geared with more dedication towards examination.

Talking about Indian Cricket team, sometimes they win and sometimes they lose, winning and losing with a same team on same ground having same players. Why two results are coming when teams are same. Because when India won their match there was a dedicated effort and when they lost, efforts were less dedicated than the opposite team.

So golden rule for successful person in life is that you have to work dedicatedly in field of your subject, everybody has to put dedication to get success, the person who put more effort comes out as successful man.

How to develop dedication – Dedication comes from how well you are prepared for situation and how much effort you will going to give to that situation to handle.

We have seen mother cradling baby on her lap and trying to make him sleep for hours. She puts her dedicated efforts to make him sleep i.e. they sing song, make surrounding peaceful, give him swinging efforts and everything she can do for him so you can see the degree of involvement there, so to achieve any goal in life your involvement should be there and this involvement is called as dedication.

You just compare those 5-6 months of mother's life in caring her newborn child that is what we called as dedication.

With child she sleeps and with child she wakes up, affection, concentration, attention, she gives to her child is comparable to dedication.

When you are working in your professional life, you have to give a mother's new born child caring treatment to your work i.e. attention, care, concentration and everything you have to achieve your goals keeping a mother's image always in your mind. Don't leave any work in between by thinking that this is impossible because when you are leaving that work, it may be in the stage of final touches and only 1% efforts are more required to finish it and if you leave it now then you again have to go back to 0 and start it again to reach at 100. So try to accumulate all you have while working on assignments.

I will tell you a very simple example of dedication.

There are millions of vehicles on the road always moving from one place to another, almost all the person reaches their destination, but few make accidents in between due to lack of concentration while driving and few are late in reaching their destination.

So it happens in our daily working also that generally we all finish our routine work, few are unable to finish it is because of lack of efforts and few complete it late. So this all come from how dedicatedly you are pursuing your work.

Every individual on this earth is always in a midway of situation, that is having surrounding and we have to sail out of it to reach at destination at other situation and surroundings. When we are facing any situation then we also have to come out of situation anyway to make life moving. For this we have to make a point that, we have to perform all our deeds with all our dedication that we have, as every deed is taking us out of a situation, it is comparative that some situations are hard for someone and some are easy for some one.

So you add dedication as part of your personality because we have lot of potential inside us but we do not use our potential (dedicated efforts) to solve problems. If we start using it we will always emerge as winner.

I strongly recommend dedication to your personality because we all have this feeling once or many times in life that if we have done it once more or if we have given it one more try, we could have finished it. So never leave things in haste for future things. Current things on which you are working may prove more useful to you than the future thing. Sometimes we quit certain important decisions in life that can change our life also.

So make a point in life to give your all strength to a situation and if you are still not be able to make it, analyze it with your capabilities and if at all, you think you can make it, put your efforts because most of the things are achieved on comparative efforts put nu others and on level of your preparedness.

If you are determined to do some work you shape your personality as per that work you're your attitude, confidence, decision making leadership qualities and vision etc. all the personality tool starts favoring you. So for achieving things be determined and proceed.

GOAL

Driving life to achieve certain objective is goal. Goals are short terms and long terms. Goal changes from time to time also. Everyone is having some ultimate goals to achieve.

Goals are very important in human life, it is different goals only which an individual always try to achieve throughout his life. Generally we consider only those things as goals, which are having big impact on life, but goals are something, which we daily achieve, and after achieving set new goals. Achieving goal always gives happiness, satisfaction and motivation.

Setting of goals are very important process because after knowing destination a person can move towards it to achieve it.

So first we understand about goal, it gives direction to life, and if there is no direction in life how can you know where you have to reach in your life and what you have to do.

As we have discussed that there are few ultimate goals of person for which person work whole of his life to reach. These ultimate goals can also be achieved when you achieve daily goals in your life.

So the process of achieving daily routine goals leads to fulfillment of long-term objectives, which in turn make us capable of achieving our ultimate goal.

In a football match there are two teams and both team ultimate goal is to win the match, for winning match they have to play in a manner where they can take football towards goal post direction of opposite team and score goal. So this is again a goal of team players to score goals. So it is goal post only, which is giving direction to player to play. Imagine if there is no goal post there, then there is no direction and everyone plays without any direction, means game would lead nowhere. So every individual has to set goals and work towards it to make his life successful.

Everyone wants to be successful in life, but is everyone has to set his goal and working to achieve it. Answer will be no in most of the cases.

Some people have goals of leading a successful professional life, for which they work in office to achieve all the short-term goals that are required to be successful professional.

While setting your goals it should be understood that goals can only be achieved by working towards them, it is not that you mere think to be a 'Doctor' and you become doctor you have to work to achieve admission in medical college then only you can become a doctor.

How to set Goals and achieve them?

Goal setting starts from the birth of a child. His parents set goal for him, and want to make him doctor engineer, etc when he grown up.

Then with time child starts growing and started going to school and soon reaches 10th and then 12th standard. These are turning points in everyone's individual life. Here you have to set a goal for your life because once you make decision, then you cannot turn back as time comes back.

At this time few people are very sure what they have to do in their life and they stick to it because they were totally aware of surroundings. But believe me I have notice that at this turning point most of the people are confused to set their goals. At this stage, do not take decision in haste, take your own time to take decision because this decision will going to affect whole of your future.

So from school and college days goal setting is very important process in life, the early you understand the path of your life it is better to achieve your goals.

For this I request parents, teachers, society and everyone who has awareness about environment, please make kids aware of their surroundings when they are in their schools, by having some extra sessions for briefing them about available career avenues in society and what all are advantages and disadvantages of it. A school going child decide his goal from his limited exposure where he is only having book knowledge and some preconceived thoughts of his surroundings. So this ultimate goal should be decided by lot of patience and awareness because you are choosing your way and you have to choose a right way.

You might have met many people in your life who says that they are not happy with what they are doing, one very important thing while setting goal in your life is that no field is good or bad, if you have potential and liking towards that field, you can create a miracle out of it.

Without a proper goal in your life you cannot be successful.

After your school and college days are over & you enter your professional life, then also you have to set your goals to give direction to life. Here persons who have decided there goals on their will in schools and colleges are already ahead by few years in achieving the ultimate goal of life than the person who are deciding their goals now in professional life.

So it is always better to decide goal in your life as early as possible.

If we see a holistic view on this earth then we will find everyone wants to live life happily and satisfactorily. This is only possible when you have achieve your predefined goal by achieving short-term goals in every small interval of time.

Commitment   12

Promise to keep our words at workplace with others and with own self is called commitment. Commitment is key of getting respect and love from others. It is required everywhere in life to achieve success and achievements. It is our commitment to society that we live life by helping others and not creating disturbance and vice versa & on this principle all the societies works. Our commitment at workplace is to complete all the work in hand on time and help other's in working. Commitment is to manage our own self with discipline to achieve all the desires in proper time to avoid stress, frustration and unhappiness.

Commitment has lot of advantages if fulfilled, if not fulfilled then it also give you image of a person who take things on granted and we cannot achieve success.

Let's understand self-commitment first, to achieve success in life it is very clear that we have to define our goal as early as possible in our life, for defining the goals early in life we require self-commitments for achieving it otherwise setting goal is easy but achieving goal is not possible.

In today's world people already landed on moon and achieved heights of Mount Everest. This is goal of them, which was backed by deep commitments. Commitments is driving force, which sits inside your soul and control your action. It is a source of inspirations through which efforts are made to achieve success.

If today I set my goal to be a successful industrialist and I am not committed from inside then I am fooling myself. So without commitment you cannot achieve self-success.

Commitment at work place are your professional life commitments and with others are your interpersonal commitments.

It is our commitments with our employer to reach office on time, so this is understood, this is not to be said again and again, and so many commitments a person has to take care while moving in society because they are expected from him.

How can be a person successful at his work place till he is ready to face every challenge of his professional life as opportunity to grow? So if you are committed with yourself and with your work place to grow in professional life then you search for challenges to grow rather they come to you. You on your own get challenges for yourself and get result out of them to prove your capabilities.

How to develop commitment -:

Making yourself aware about the future surrounding develops commitment. It gets developed when you understand that it is within us, but we have hidden it since long and thus we have to groom it.

Let understand it from an old example – Whenever people get into a trouble they start praying to God. Now tell me one thing how can someone stop you from praying. But you do not feel that as requirement, so you do not pray. When you come in a situation where you require help or there is risk of failure, then you start praying that to for whole of your life. So commitment is within us but we do not take it out till it is required, we only commit ourselves when we have a feeling of failure or it is required.

People who take alcohol and cigarette are very happy having both, but when medical science suggest them to avoid these things otherwise they will suffer severe consequences, than they commit themselves avoid them.

Same way if at our workplace when our boss gets angry with us due to non-performance then we get commit ourselves to perform.

So we can see commitment is within our own self but we human have got tendency to only use things when they are required otherwise we keep them idle.

Let me put in this way-

People take money from bank as capital to start business and work hard on that to achieve success. Similarly inside your own capital is hidden, you just give yourself a thought, that what all things you are doing can be done in better way & what else you are not doing presently, which you can add in your life which will give you happiness.

Believe me, if we commit from our self that we will live happy life from future onwards no one in this world can dare to make us unhappy because we change all our situation and surrounding as per requirement. Our attitude, change and our thoughts will drive us to a different world of happiness.

Why it always happened all of a sudden in our life, we say to ourselves "This thing is really fabulous and giving me lot of happiness. I really don't know it is so close by me"

This is common sentence with everyone when we see or feel any good thing around, this is something which you found on requirement, but if you have tried it you could have got this earlier also but you were not committed for that, so you never tried for it also. So many wonderful things we are able to find in our life are when we make commitment in life to explore the possibilities.

We only realize the other part of grass as green when we failed to reach the other side i.e. we only realize the happiness of getting promotion when we failed to receive it and then we commit ourselves to achieve the same.

So it is discipline within yourself, which you have to develop to control your activities and get the result out of them.

If we make a commitment today of exploring our self for 15 minutes daily, then we see how fast, we come to know that we were using just half the potential of what we were having. We only start working with our left hand when right hand get fractured. Why, because left was not required to perform activities in life. Means still at workplace we are having scope to produce more output than usual, we just have to explore our self and commit to do better things.

Nobody on this earth come with an assured future, some people has to maintain their legacy and some have to build their future. They are able to achieve success only, when they are committed for that and already disciplined their life as per requirements, so when everyone has to discipline his life then why not today onwards we all commit to build a better future and prosper ourselves

Process *13*

Different steps which we follow to reach to the end result of any work, is called process i.e. knowingly or unknowingly every person is following some process to achieve the result.

Process making are always useful to individuals, business and at any other set up. If you have set a process then you do not waste daily in pondering on same issue.

So we can also define process as predefined way of working i.e. you are visualizing your situations and surroundings far before they actually happened to avoid any difficulties and problems.

We have seen in many work places that there is a daily meeting to address all the issues and deriving solutions for them, daily meeting takes many hours and to implement their results again take few more days. So generally we make processes when we actually face any difficulties and problems at workplace but processes are to be predefined to save time, money and stress.

In my career I have worked with many companies, I tell you about the difference between companies with processes. Two companies started business together and started working to achieve their set objectives and goal.

Company A was the company which behaves in facing all the problems at the same time when they actually comes and Company B believes in setting all the process before they actually starts. So they laid down all the processes and documented them before actual start of business.

When both the companies comes in operation phase, Company A has to stop it operations again and again to reach at a solution and further to that to avoid same difficulty not to arrive, they have to frame a process for that, finally, that company turns sick. But Company B was running successfully with all its potential because in that company every employee know what all are the processes and how to tackle every work situation.

So we can understand from this example that to avoid any hindrance in our future, work plans, process is highly recommended solution.

You might have seen many persons confused at their work places and in personal life because they are puzzled with the problems due to lack of any process, you want to handle any work your efforts just go on increasing like anything without process.

Generally all works which we perform in our daily life and at workplace all are generally repetitive and monotonous in nature so can be well achieved by setting a process.

When we all have to almost perform same job daily then why we do not make a process, which can be best effective with least time consuming. Let's understand this with Example:-

Everyone on this earth has to file the official papers that are of his use in future course of action. We require papers which are related to our income, bank statements, telephone nos., address etc. but any time when we require them for any purpose, we do not find them on places because we are not following any process to keep storing them or arranging them in proper manner.

How to make processes in life?

If you are very puzzled in life, you are confused in life, you are not getting time for doing anything for yourself, it is only work, work and work all the time, people are not happy with you as you are unable to satisfy anyone. So this is time for you for process making in personal & professional life.

You just sit on a place and analyze for 1 hour only what has gone wrong in your life which are creating so many problems. You will find everything is ok except due to lack of processes you are getting puzzled and you have reached to the stage of depression and you are unable to make yourself happy and this is a time to make your life simple.

When you analyze your life, you will find that all the works, which are repetitive in nature they are taking mainly all the time due to which, you are not able to perform other works. I.e. while going to office always you do not find many things, which are required in office. You have to search for data, for doing same type of work, you are using different approaches because you have not made processes, you are wasting your time in talking on irrelevant issues and you might be giving more time on lunch breaks and tea breaks.

So all the work which are repetitive required process from today itself, you will find you were able to have much more time than earlier.

You have to understand that all the people who were successful and the persons who were unsuccessful both had same amount of time in their life, but some people have made wonders out of their 24 hours in a day and some people are still struggling to get some time for themselves.

You might have observed that many people on same positions in offices, having same work have different behavior. One is very good and social, enjoy every part of life and other person always in very frustrating mood, cursing life for not having time and growth in life because he has not formulated processes to work.

Let's experiment this from today itself, you take out your copy pen and write all the work which you have to perform today. It looks very simple but mostly people do not plan their routine activities and this causes unnecessarily waste of time. So we have to make a process of making a chart/plan of daily activities.

For making process we have to do nothing great, rather we just have to analyze that all the works which we are doing at work place or in personal life can be managed in more efficient way or not.

Concentration 14

Our mind is very dynamic in nature, whenever we are working on something and try to put all our thoughts in one direction, our mind get diverted towards many other things.

While working on some work, if you are able to manage your thoughts, so that they do not divert in other directions and you can work on that particular situation by only analyzing the thoughts which are similar to that situation is called concentration.

When we concentrate, we get into deeper thoughts and can come out with a solution of difficult situation easily. Concentration has capabilities to block all the thought which are destructive in nature and which can hinder you from reaching to any solution.

Concentration is a tool, which can develop, power of thinking deeply so that we emerge with different solutions of different situation.

It is basically main achievement and goal of meditation process also. In all the meditation processes we have to work towards a thoughtless mind, where no thoughts can hinder us and we reach to a position of consciousness to enlighten ourselves.

In meditation we make our mind thoughtless, so that from free mind we can think in a better way on difficult situation without have any prejudice feeling of past. We reach to a situation, where without any efforts we can concentrate and come out with solutions.

This is advisable to everyone on this earth that you should know how to control all those feeling which are coming to your mind, because these are the thoughts, which always have a big impact on your behavior and you react accordingly.

Why generally it happened like that, in a meeting people do not play songs and other entertainment resources, because that is a place where people are accumulated to drive a solution and if you start listening to music and other things how can you concentrate on issues.

Why important discussions are not taken at a noisy market place with lot of crowd around, because you cannot concentrate.

Why senior persons are generally given a peaceful place, so that they can resolve problem without hindrances.

Why people go to aloof places while writing on something, which require deep thoughts.

All these things requires concentration and if you are solving problems by some concentration you will always get better results.

Generally concentration is a feature of personality, which some good students learn from their school and college days & this is the reason why they also achieve success. Sometimes we also try to concentrate on situation and ended up with headache this is because we have not develop a practice of giving deep thoughts to situation.

Many a times we did not remember old things, this is because, either we have not listen that thing earlier with concentration or today we are unable to concentrate, so it is a main driver of your memory system also.

On very easy situation you are unable to suggest a solution but your fellow mate comes out with an excellent solution and you think that if you have given few seconds more to think about it, this will also be your solution, but at that time it does not strike your mind, this all is concentration only.

How to develop it?

Concentration is an inner power through which you can control your thoughts and think on a particular situation deeply for longer time without any hindrance.

Some people have in born capabilities of thinking problem deeply with free mind but if we are unable to develop it then we are not late for it as it's something which is within yourself only and you have to explore it.

You can concentrate on daily issues if you develop personality traits like avoiding stress and ignoring irrelevant activities, which really does not mean to us, and involvement in them only make our attitude negative.

Secondly you can also practice 5 minutes meditation, which will help you in developing conciseness and enlighten yourself.

In morning I usually sit in a comfortable place with aim of making mind thoughtless, I do meditation. I sit with my eyes closed, as soon as I start meditating thoughts starts coming to me randomly, I do not obstruct any thought rather I welcome them and say them to go after some time. Thoughts comes to me for 5-10 minutes but I never obstruct any thought. I simply welcome them and finally allow them to go, while welcoming thoughts I have in back of my mind that I also have to make my mind thoughtless, so letting them go is also not very difficult. Here we have to be clear that we should not have to obstruct any thought, otherwise it will give us stress and we lead to headache. So follow this process for a month or two you will find a progress while your meditation and number of thoughts starts reducing and will take less time to move from restlessness mind to calm mind. After reaching to the stage of calm mind you plan all your important activities for the day and business. This process will give you concentration will be deep enough to bring best out of your capabilities.

In other words I can also say that, in busy life you have to take out 10-15 minutes for yourself, where you have to position yourself that where you are and where you have to reach.

Let me tell you a good practice is never late, when you come to know about it, learn it, the mistake you are doing is that, after knowing a good practice you are not learning it by thinking you are late, this approach will lead you to pessimism.

So learn to concentrate on all works that are desired from you and you can see that concentration is within yourself and you just have to explore it and dig it out.

Comparison   15

Analyzing self with other's wealth, status and belongings or in other words to compare everything of ours with everything of others is called as comparison.

This is a very common practice, which we can see in every individual. People generally compare themselves with others and get frustrated. This comparison is very common among businesses, office mates, housewives, students and nearly most of the human beings.

We have seen generally people frustrated because they are not having what others are having. People have enough money for them still they are not happy because others are having more money. There is list of such comparison that exist in a society & a person do them on daily basis. If we understand life then we find comparisons are required also the growth because through that only we get motivation and motivation is key factor for growth, but here I am talking about those comparisons where human being really get inspired and try to achieve something through that because these healthy comparisons are very rare in society. In most of the cases person compare them self with person who are ahead of them and start cursing their failure instead to get motivation from it, for growth.

Why Comparison in Society?

Man is a social animal, everything people sees from the perspective of others, he did not see whether his objectives are achieved or not & in many senses he want to prove himself in front of others to gain respect. Comparisons are there because when a person is working with other person then he also has to compare himself with others in terms of growth.

We all grow in a society where we all have to fix our goal that we have to achieve, the goals which we want to achieve must be achieved by someone earlier also, and this is why we are comparing our self with others to achieve that same goal.

Comparisons are also made by societies like many of your relatives when come to your home, they have common curiosity of knowing what you are doing and what common friends known to both of you are doing, and they make comparisons about progress.

On meeting with old friends, their common question is about what you are doing & what other friend are doing. Even parents compare their two children.

We decide good & bad on comparative scale only.

So everything around us is having comparison within some aspect or the other and these are comparison which man faces daily in his life, so he develops a personality where he also start comparing self with others in everything what he possess.

Is Comparison Good or Bad

Comparison with others are always good if it gives you good feeling of motivation and happiness, you should always avoid those situation and surrounding where through comparison stress is generated. Avoid all those situation where you feel that comparison will give you negative thoughts. But there are some situations where we cannot avoid comparison i.e. at the time of annual appraisal in company or during examination results. So be ready to face it.

Always learn from comparisons to achieve more, because if you were compared with someone and others p are evaluated superior then you take this situation as opportunity to know all the things which you are lacking and try to learn the things and emerge as more powerful leader.

It is very simple that when you can't beat them, join them and if still they are better than us then follow them to learn things because you will find very few people in life who are really having talents.

If someone is rated or compared better than you, it does not harm your personality, because in this world everyone is having individual identity, no one can be superior than you, till you accept it on your own and willing to learn from him.

While talking about self-comparisons, it should be always avoided if it is leading to jealousy and depression.

These all comparison feeling comes to our mind when we did not use our complete balance of mind to analyze situation, let's take a very common example. Generally people have feeling that they have more intelligence and qualities but still they are earning less than their counter part.

My dear friend whole world is open to explore your personality, if you feel that the company you are working is not recognizing your qualities and you get feeling of depression, you have whole world to explore, if you really have the more intelligence and qualities one day you will find better job as per your capabilities.

It is simply worthless to sit in isolation and always think that why he is better than us. Don't let these feeling ride your mind because these are parasites and they are coming to you due to all the situation and surrounding you have faced earlier in your life, you are also no way less capable than your counterpart but you have developed feelings which are making you depressed and giving stress.

So we will make this point in life that compare things only for motivation and learnings if something is giving us stress we will avoid it and analyze our self for better tomorrow.

Relationship 16

Relationship can be defined in two ways – Relationship with our current surroundings, when we meet daily at our work place and in our day to day life and second is our old relations which we left behind because when life moves, we also have to move with life and many new relation get establishes. In old relation we can also consider relation which are inborn relation with relatives.

So life moves like this only, we meet many people daily, we come in contact with many people, we establish relations with them as per surroundings and situations, but as life move everybody has to move, so we also move in exploring new opportunities and challenges where our surrounding are changing always and we meet new people who come in contact.

If we want to recollect names, addresses and phone no. of all those people whom we met earlier in life then it is not easy for us to collect them. It is also practically not possible also, but due you not think that all these old relation really matters in life.

I think there is not a single person on this earth, whose surrounding have not produced successful person, definitely there are successful people from your surroundings also but today you don't know where they are what they are doing because when we go ahead for new relations we totally forget most of our old relations.

It is really not possible for us to keep record or data of every person whom we met in our life, but we can keep some data of all the potential people whom we met in our life and whenever we get time or occasions, we should have to wish them or pay our regards to them depending on situation.

If we are calling someone without any intention to ask any favor from him that person always feel delighted.

You can always add this practice to your personality, this always help in future course of life.

So relationship is a side by side exercise in this busy life where we keep track and record of all those persons, who are not in daily touch with us but we remember them on occasions and events so that they are always as support for us in time of need.

Let me give one example how it works – I started my professional career by working with a Finance company and was handling the profile of car financing, car financing is real good job to do because car is mostly a dream for everyone and you are arranging money for that which make your customer delighted. So while working with this company I have made this practice of maintaining database of all the Customers whom I financed the cars.

After a year I took a job change and went to Europe for another job, I do not find my new job challenging and I started disliking my job there, but how can I return home back till I am not having any secured job in my hand. So I started searching in data base of my old relation which I have made in old company and found some of the head of HR whom I have financed the car. But after financing the car, we were not in touch from last one year. So I was also feeling slightly shy for asking them help straight way. Still, I thought to send e-mail, to wish till I make up my mind to ask for help.

I mailed them and wish them my regards, if I have mailed to 10 people on 3 reverted, so now I am quite sure of that if I asked for help with these three they will help me, so I write same mail to all the three asking for a job in India.

One of the HR head replied very respectfully that we are always looking for energetic person like you and any time you are welcome.

So this is how relation works, some time when you are in a very difficult situations, your relations help to come out of them.

Second type of relationship are current relationships, these relationship make us happy, satisfied and motivated in daily life and that finally leads to a life of successful manager.

How to develop relationships?

A person develops relations whenever he/she interact with a people for some official work and for some personal work. Now it is totally on us how we are going to take that meeting as, if we want to develop connection then through that meeting we should build long lasting relation.

For developing relations it is not only one personality trait that counts, you have to develop versatile personality to create relations. First thing which you always have to keep in your mind is that you always have to yourself in front of a person. So while interacting with a person you should always be very humble and as you start understanding the person you change yourself as per his requirements.

People always look for qualities in a person which are compatible to them while making relation. So all is qualities which a person wants in you. In every situation and surroundings we always can judge the thoughts of a person by our developed personality and has to interact in a way that person should feel delighted.

No one on this earth want to have relations with ruthless, jealous and Self-obsessed. Everyone want relation that they can rely on in time of need. And if you have very harmless, humble and a good listener attitude you can develop good relations.

Generally everyone want someone on whom they can rely and relations should not break trust. So there are many qualities, which you have to develop for successful relationships.

Finally the key word for successful relations are – equipped your personality with such personality traits through which your personality get shaped in a way where everyone feel delighted in your presence.

Professional Growth

17

Gradual surge in life is called Growth. When we move ahead in life in terms of money, career, position, achievements and etc., until we reach at our final goal.

Today every individual is working towards something, some individuals who have set their goals they are working to achieve their goals and others who have not set their goals they are working through opportunities coming their way and by chance. Means everyone has to work in his life to achieve the required desires what he or she is having. When we work, we measure ourselves with different parameters, like 3 years ago we were where and now we are on which position, how much money we have saved in our professional life etc. Every individual set his own parameter to analyze himself that where he is now, this is called as growth.

Every person has different growth plans in life and when person grow as per his plan he feel motivated and satisfied.

So we can also say growth as parameter of measuring the person's achievement.

To grow in life you have to set your goals and plan them ahead, because till the time you do not know what you want to achieve you cannot achieve them. So for growing ready with you plan as early as possible in life.

Generally growth is comparative and relative in nature so be careful that comparative nature of growth will not give you any stress at workplace.

We have seen in our life that many of our mates are growing fast and some are growing slow, that is what shows the nature of growth is comparative, this is why we have derive inference that some of my friends are growing slow and some are fast. Some times when we are more ambitious and we compare our self with person who are growing faster than we generates stress within us.

We have to avoid this stress because we do not know in what surrounding he is growing and what surroundings we have to grow, if both surroundings are different that we cannot compare growth on one person with another. So these type of stresses are not required. Comparing two person with each other of different surrounding is not relevant, which is more clear with this example – Sagar and Ashish were very good friends, they completed their college days together and started doing job. Sagar who was having relatives in United States went there and start his job and Ashish start working in India only, Sagar secured a job of 100,000 US dollars/Annum and Ashish got a job of Rs 12 lac/annum (USD 18000) in India. If you compare these two job Sagar is getting very high salary because he is living in a country where surroundings are permitting employer to pay him such a high salary but Ashish is not getting such high salary because he is getting as per his surroundings. Though they both are of same college, where they usually score moreover same grades also.

So sometimes people grow due to virtue of their surroundings, where they have not contributed much and sometimes people who are trying very hard also unable to grow because surroundings cannot permit them to do so. Surrounding can be group of people also and it can be as big as economy of country also. So it is very clear that we have to analyze our growth taking all these factors in consideration.

To be successful in life we all have to set our growth plan very early in live in analyzing our potential, for judging our potential we are the best judge. Let me take growth from micro to macro level now, every country publish their GDP growth, inflation growth and how much forex will grow. So if we see that on macro level also everything is classified in growth terms and that to well in advance, same like an individual should also have to analyze his growth needs.

Let's understand why growth is important in life – Growth is very important factor of life because it is growth only through which you are accepted and achieve high status in society.

Growth is a multi-dimensional process, individual enhances their capabilities in all the fields related with their work environment, and this enhancement also give them better growth options.

Why all the times everyone talk about growth in life only, why things are linked with growth, why growth is consider so important factor, there is reason for that. If I take you way back in our old civilization, you can see there were limited development as such, people are having very limited scope for their work areas. You don't even think of all the modern amenities which we are today part of and still driving them in new direction, this is what we call as growth, that with gradual pace civilization has grown in all these past years and today we reached at level which if we compare it with our old civilization, we really cannot believe that is this possible.

With the pace this world is growing, we also have to grow our self, as this world grow in multidimensional direction, we also have to grow our skills like that to be successful in this world. Can you think of a person who was isolated from this earth from last 50 years, if suddenly comes on this earth back? How he will cope with this changed world. I think he will be puzzled to understand all these vast changes that took place in last 50 years.

This is how your life works, you have to adapt yourself with all the chances which are taking place in your surroundings to keep the pace of your growth with this earth. If you are unable to grow yourself with the pace of surroundings, you will be obsolete and your skill demand will be reduced. So be sure that you on a right track and growing with a pace, which is faster than your surroundings to achieve success.

Don't misunderstand growth with glamour, growth also have different perception, like for a politician growth may be to become President of nation, for actor it may be to become superstar, but for a farmer it may be to produce more than that what he has produce last year, same like for a student it may be to score more marks than what he has secured in last examination. So growth got different perception from person to person but in actual sense growth is setting of your target as early stage as possible and start moving towards it with a gradual pace so that you can achieve in the time frame which you have decide. It may be possible sometimes you achieve your goals in life faster because you were supported by your surroundings, but still you have to grow yourself with changing world to keep yourself update and finally we can also code growth as satisfaction which person gets in moving towards his goal when gets gradual successes.

So be ready to grow and don't get depressed by your negative surroundings because your growth is totally driven by you, your positive surrounding and other support systems.

Objectivity 18

We use different approaches to solve different problems. We have discussed earlier also, while solving problem most of the time we take decisions as per the thoughts, which have been developed throughout our life.

Objectivity means to see every problem, which comes across to us with holistic view. We have to see it with all facts and figures that are applicable to that problem according to today's situation and what will be its future impact.

In other words objectivity is the analysis of situation as per current surroundings and not to be dominated by all the preconceived thoughts, which we are having in our mind.

Generally people follows a herd mentality that it is happening like this from so long, so now also it should happen like this only.

We generally forget that with this changing world every problem should be treated with a new original solution, which will help us in solving it much better.

All the thoughts that you are having regarding tackling different situations of life are always a tool in your hand to see the dimensions, type and requirement of problem.

But do not mix your solution with the dominance of some irrelevanr thoughts. When you use objective approach you really think out of box and come out with solution, which is really an invention.

Generally people do their work in the style suggested to them and year to year that work move in same style of working, someday a person comes and put his objective mind to do that work and reduce time, labor and cost to just half. So this is what we call an objective thinking by producing a unique solution.

We are not saying that objective solution cannot be achieved by your pre-conceived thoughts, it can be achieved if you are having right perception about the problem. Generally every one perceives problem in his own way, so the best way is to use your perception as a tool and see what factors are effecting current situation and surroundings before arriving at any result.

The normal way or routine way of working i.e. where we get all the inputs from past and finish our work on the guidance laid out by our experienced and senior persons or the thoughts which we have developed. But do you think this will help you in growing further and achieve new heights. When you all think and do same what earlier people have done then development of whole society will stop. Earlier also there were many people who have took problems from objective way and come out with real solutions for which today we are benefited, same we have to do, so that coming generation will be benefited.

So objectivity is to come out with the best solution for the present times by putting apart all the preconceived thoughts that we are having.

Let's take some example of objectivity.

It was a common notion before Sir Isaac Newton discovered gravity, that everything will fall down to earth and will not fly to sky without knowing the reason, if Sir Isaac Newton should also thought in a same way then he would not have come out with the solution of force of Gravity which exist on this earth and pulls everything towards it. After knowing this fact many inventions were done, because everybody was sure of the fact that there is some constant force, which will work. So it is the objective mind of Newton only which come out with such a solution that has created history.

Money 19

Everyone on this earth requires money. Money is driving force for almost every individual on this earth. Money is having a special characteristic, more it is with a person he wants more. So for money, everyone is very particular and chasing money.

The power of money is immense and anything can be purchased by money, there are few abstract things which sometimes are not possible through money also, but in this material world they are very few.

We have seen people working daily, day to night because of money only and money gives them all the luxury and requirement of their daily life.

I am not saying earning money is bad rather, it is always good to earn money because it gives you all what is required to live a peaceful life. If I see a general observation, people having money are more satisfied (if we talk only of basic need) than person who are having relatively less money.

Generally human behavior has a typical quality of comparing each other which we have discussed earlier also, so in terms of money there is comparison, because money is one of the biggest factor to achieve every required thing in life but sometimes in earning more money we simply lose all the charm of life.

Let's see some practical things in life about money – I have experience that people living in village can easily run their expenses of household in Rs. 10000/-/Month (taking example of average family size of 4). While in metros like Mumbai and Delhi for running your house hold expenses you require Rs 50,000 or more and in countries like US in New York even Rs. 100,000 is even not substantial amount to run your family expenses.

So as you move towards high standard of living your expenses are going to increase and you require more money to suffice your needs.

If we relocate same family from a small town to Mumbai – they require more money (Including Basic needs also because they are costly in Mumbai) and if I take same family from Mumbai to a small town their expenses will come down.

So in general, people spend money as per their surroundings, we want to live with same status as others are living, (exclude our basic needs) we require money to match our living standards with the people who consist our surrounding.

And in doing so, if we do not earn as per our expectation, we develop stress which affects us so badly that our attitude towards life change.

We all have to understand that we are earning money for our self. If we are able to fulfill our requirement with that then there is no requirement of any tension because if others are earning more or less, it practically does not affect us because neither they take money from us nor we will give money to them. So all these are the just thoughts regarding money that makes us tense.

Let us understand one more example – You all have observed that in our life as we start earning more our expenses also goes on increasing. We are able to easily manage our self in half the salary earlier and now double the salary is not enough to meet the expenses. (Netting of cost of inflation). We have to understand this, that with our growth and progress our requirement also increases because we have move to higher standard of living. But these all requirements which we are increasing has no end, so we have to keep in mind that after fulfillment of our basic requirements, no man can earn that much that he can fulfill all his desires.

Today may be I am having stress due to someone I know who earn more than me, same people also must be knowing many people who must be earning more than him.

So there is no limit for money, while talking about money you have to explain your mind that containment is best policy.

Earning money through exploring yourself – Generally if we see around us, people do various jobs to earn money, from these jobs some people earn more money and some earn less. The people who earn more are basically those who may their interest and qualities as their career. Let's understand this also – we all are blessed by many qualities by God, but for whole of life we are unable to understand what all qualities we are having and if we are able to understand them also still we are reluctant in making our career in that field due to lack of confidence and vision.

Generally everyone on this earth wants to live as a mediocre only and want to get place in existing running eco-system rather than to work on their original qualities, as to make our skills salable in market as there is a risk of failure.

Here I congratulate all those who have identified their skills in early life only and work on that and today really come out with a success. These people are having all the guts to take risk to develop their skills and then earn through their skills only.

If great cricket players in their early age were not able to identify their skills of cricket then today they must not be that much successful person.

So every person has some or the other skills but we have always fear of choosing them as career option because the success chances are less and we move to a path which is not an interest for us but through with we can at least earn substantial and live happily without any risk.

There are other people also who are very successful in life and earning very well that is because they are very much aware of their personality and their needs.

Jealousy 20

When one person does not feels happy with growth of other person, it is jealousy. Jealousy can be for anything when there is comparing attitude. But jealousy is the biggest and most dangerous parasite, which eats human personality and hinder its growth.

Jealousy is a personality trait, which exists in every human being, but the intensity differs.

But every human being has to try to control it at the best.

I have experienced many people who are highly talented but they simply spoil their career due to their attitude of jealousy.

Jealousy is basically a feeling of un satisfaction, which grips us. We feel, what we have is not enough for us and we started comparing with others. When we are already under depression and negative thoughts, then we feel all the things, which others possess, are better than us and thus we come under the feeling of frustration and unhappiness.

How Jealousy get Generated –

Let me be very clear on this that if you are jealous with someone there is nothing wrong in other person, it is something wrong at your end only. You are not happy with your present position in this world or there is something, which you are lagging behind, and others are having.

It is also very clear that normally in this world it is not very easy to avoid jealousy attitude completely. Where everything is comparative with each other jealousy attitude generally comes in human feeling.

Jealousy is commonly between the close friends or it is between our known circles. A person is not jealous of a person when he did not know him at all.

Development of jealousy again pertain to human characteristics where he always see himself better than others and in return want maximum from the society.

Sometimes it is good to see yourself as better; because it gives you motivation but do not ignore others fully, may be someone has some good qualities which may pull him up.

Or it is vice-versa when a person feels himself inferior from others generate jealousy attitude.

There is one very good definition of jealousy also – when a group of people want to achieve same goal they compete with each other till their group achieves its goal. In this person with balance mind develop feeling of competitiveness with each other while some with unsatisfied feeling generates feeling of jealousy.

How to Control

The only way to control jealousy is to content your own self. Till the time you are not satisfied and happy with your own self the feeling of jealousy comes to your mind.

For self-satisfied many of you have to understand all these personality traits which we are discussing in this book, through this you will come to understand that jealousy can only hinder our path and never makes us fast to achieve our objectives.

Again for understanding of self-content man, you have to understand the situation, surrounding and thoughts process. And you have to understand this that there are certain situations where you cannot drive surroundings and when you are a part of a surrounding which is driven by someone else, you develop some thoughts, which are also influenced by others and these thoughts may give you different personality traits. And one of them is feeling of jealousy also, but you have to understand it that any feeling which is giving you stress, when you are working with your fellow worker, avoid it or analyze it may be that you are taking problem from some other angle& it is simple for other end.

I want to tell you a simple trick which you should have to apply at your work place to understand whether you are in grip of jealousy or not.

You just analyze your interaction with all your fellow mates, now see how many give you delight and feeling of security when talking to them, all these friends are good and jealousy factor is not there and if this feeling of delight and security is not there while working with someone it means there is some jealousy vice-versa.

Friends

Friend is a person who gives you feeling of security, delight and happiness when you are around him or talking to him or there is a very common definition of friend – A friend in need is a friend indeed. If someone is helping you in all those situations that you find difficult to come out and due to other persons help you are able to get rid of problem than, other person is showing quality of friendship.

Friendship is necessity of life. Friends give us happiness and delight from time to time. Sometime friends change whole life by doing many things for us.

Why friends are so required: - you might have observed in your life that there are some movement where you require someone to share your views and ideas, someone who can share your sorrows, thoughts and you can depend on him to take decisions. These all things we only get from friends.

If we see a life of a person he always require friends to stand his career and growth. When you are a kid your father and mother are your best friends who takes care of everything that is required by you.

As we grow we go to school, we make friends, there whom we interact daily and come in use of each other on time of requirements. Similarly we have in college some friends.

We have many friends in our professional life and as we grow further our wife, children also become our friends i.e. in every field of life we are making friends and taking help and give help to them.

You can see friends in your parents who only want to give you, never want to take anything from you. Friends also fulfill our self-esteem needs, they help us in keeping our motivation alive.

Why you find a person always cheerful, who is having lot of friends and vice versa because with all these friends we typically fulfill our need of to be expected with each other.

Do and don'ts of a friend:-

Friends are always good and helpful for us, but some time we think a person is a friend but he is just using us or he is having some other intention except friendship. We have to very much beware of all these peoples.

Rather it is always better to have 2-3 good friends than to have 100 friend. Sometimes 2-3 good friends contribute more than army of friends.

If you analyze your life, you have met 100's of people, but if we see there were only 4-5 people whom you really can trust and call them as friend this is with every human being.

Whenever or wherever you move, you meet many people. After meeting with people when they come close to you, you know more about them, here you can judge that with whom you can go ahead with as a friend, who is more compatible with you, because friendship is two side affair, it cannot be possible by one way interaction.

But this is also true that no person is good or bad, so while doing friendship it is not that he cannot be my friend because he is bad, because may be some other person whom we are not friend may think we are bad and some person have feeling that we are good.

So it is basically how well you can be compatible with each other is friendship.

But we have to make habit of not letting down others, not to do any distrust and never make fun of persons at public place.

We should also have to keep in mind that everyone is equal when we talk about friendship. Never talk bad word about a person when he is not present and never hinder some one's work if we are not supporting him too. Be always positive, humorous, humble, sacrificing and loving in nature to our friends. If we are following all these qualities then we have to expect these all from our friends. First you have to be good, if you want others good with you.

Motivation 22

The feeling and desire to grow and face every challenge with positive attitude is motivation.

Motivation is a personality trait, which helps human being to achieve all the heights he desire. It is motivation, which is behind every success story on this earth.

Every person today performs his daily work, student do their routine school work, professional do their work at work place and every person who is struggling to achieve success try to achieve success by working in different ways. What makes all these people working daily, it is motivation only, which makes them work daily to achieve the success.

For example, students work hard to get good result because they are motivated with people who had earlier scored good marks and they are now at new heights, same in office if person is working hard, it is motivation of promotion which is making him work harder.

So every work which we are performing there is some motivation behind that, if motivation is lost then we lose interest in work and results did not come as per expectations.

So motivation is required as catalyst to achieve success in any field.

There is always great difference of productivity and quality, if work is not been done by motivation.

Rather all the difficult works which require efforts are not possible without motivation.

If someone is unable to perform some work, you just give him motivation for achieving that work, then you can observe that his efforts will increase to double to achieve that work.

18.0.0.0.1 How Motivation Comes

Motivation is a feeling of delight and satisfaction, which comes to us to take up any task. This feeling makes us to understand about benefits we will going to have on completion of this work and then our all the driver start working in same direction to achieve success.

Sometimes motivation comes from the qualities, which we are having within like vision, leadership and never give up. Sometimes our surroundings motivate us to do some work.

If we understand our life, we will find all the works that we have given up and never started at all were because of lack of motivation only for that particular activity.

Can you imagine a work place where at end of month/designated period you are not paid and have no chances of growth further? These situation are not healthy and adverse to motivation.

So when we work, there is some motivating factor behind that work which is forcing us to complete or do that work. Let us take it from other way around, if we know what we will be going to get out of this work and if it is positive outcome, we work to achieve it otherwise we give up.

Some people who do not like their work while working did not think the objectivity of work they are doing, they did not go deep inside that work to analyze the benefit of that work, if they are also able to understand the benefits which they will going to get, then they will also start liking the work.

So, it is very simple, if person is motivated he can do any work, if he is not motivated then we first have to motivate him to achieve desire results.

Motivation comes in a human being from situation, surroundings and his thoughts.

Many people have parents and friends, who always give them motivation but there are some people who did not receive any motivation from surroundings, so we have to identify those peoples who are neglected since they born and give them motivation so that they can work better and achieve target.

Motivation comes if you praise person qualities, talk with him with respect and when you rely on him.

When a person get personal attention and his thoughts get respected he get motivation.

There are many hidden qualities of person that comes out when we give him feeling of motivation.

If you want to take 100% efficiency from a person you have to give him feeling of motivation.

How to get our own self-motivated: -

Sometimes we also come under the grip of depression and we do not feel like working, we generally do not have parents and friends always to motivate, then who can motivate us always.

For getting self-motivation you just think of all those people who are less privileged than us. After having such a little income and such a less desire they are happy than what is wrong with us. We are having everything and if some small thing go wrong also, we should work to correct it rather to get demotivated. If you analyze every problem by taking broader view, you will be motivated again.

Again we have to remember what we expect from world, is the same what we have to give this world.

For getting self-motivation we always have to think all the good causes for which we are working, i.e. for our child, parents, wife and all the dears and nears which will definitely give us self-motivation.

For self-motivation always keep in mind success and failure are parts of life, everyone has failed first and then only achieved success i.e. success is only achieved when you put more efforts than anyone else can put for it. Take example of Edison who was failed 100 hundred times before inventing the bulb. So you should always be with an attitude to achieve and then you will be always a motivated person and achieve success.

Sadness/Unhappiness 23

Whenever we are not comfortable with our feelings we feel sad. Our feelings and thoughts get uncomfortable if we are unable to achieve something desired by us. Any expectation which we were having from others did not get fulfilled or vice-versa. Any thoughts for which we are not ready but we have to accept it because that is a fact of that time, leads us to sadness and we started feeling unhappy.

It is very common phenomenon across the globe that generally people are not happy from their current position and they want to achieve something more. Every day we face certain instances, which give us feeling of unhappiness.

i.e. If we are working on some important work and we are very much involved in it and hoping to come out with good results. All of a sudden if some person told us that what we were doing is all waste and there are other methods to do it. So we feel totally shattered and our motivation changes to sadness.

It is again a daily happening where knowingly or unknowingly people hurt us and we feel rejected. The feeling of rejection gives us sadness and unhappiness and that in turns generate stress.

How to avoid sadness

When we are working on something or we are talking in some group, generally it happens that various people have different perception about the type of work we are doing or the topic on which we are debating. It is quite obvious that people have different views because every person grooms up in different surroundings and situations, so they have different thoughts. The group may accept other thoughts over yours, which may make you sad. In these situation make yourself firm on your point and place it in front of group and do not be afraid of rejection of your point.

Many people feel sad because they think that they are not accepted by the society i.e. they are unable to create a place what they deserve. Earlier also we have talked about this that these all things are comparative in nature and we don't know what things are hindering others and we are only under the illusion of green grass at other side which makes us unhappy.

If in early stage of life we analyze our capabilities and set goals as per that then we will not have to be unhappy in life. People are generally confused about their future and always think they have achieved less than what they deserve which creates the feeling of sadness.

We also have to try to develop friendship or create surroundings that give us happiness, because these surroundings give us daily thoughts and if these thoughts are of joy, fun and humor then we will come out of feeling of sadness.

Disciplined life also contributes to avoid sadness and unhappiness during our daily routine life. We our self-do some mistakes which finally leads to big damage and make us sad. This includes all the small checks that are required while doing anything.

Let's take a simple example, if you are traveling and your car gets punctured and due to your indiscipline nature you also have not kept any extra tyre in the car then this will make you sad further.

Sadness also comes to us when we develop an attitude of accepting defeat at the work places without putting serious efforts. This attitude simply crushes any human being and thus leads towards depression.

For every work which you took responsibility, you should perform it with all your efforts i.e. you always have to convince yourself that you have given your best to achieve the results. If still you are unable to achieve success then there may be some other reasons but you have tried your best.

Again some people always ponder on non-achievements in life and they develop sadness when they compare themselves with other successful people.

Again here I want to say that avoid all those comparing attitudes, which gives you stress and sadness.

One very big fact of the life is – every person whom you observe happy may be having many things to worry, but he is still laughing because he know that sadness will only eat up life and laugh can at least give him motivation to solve issues.

So why you are sad by having such a little problem. I have seen many disabled people living life with the spirit of a sportsmanship then what's wrong with you, when youare fit and capable of achieving every goal in life.

Inferiority Complex 24

Feeling of prejudice that always makes us to think that other is better than us. This feeling can be for our own self, work related things, or for our personal thing or for anything, which is ours.

This feeling eats person from inside and due to this before achieving any thing in life, he gets disappointed and went into a state of depression.

This feeling comes to a person when he is on his growth path and starts to face hurdles and defeats.

It also depends very much on your situation and surroundings and how you generate your thoughts thereafter.

Every successful man on this earth also go through many defeats in his life, but today he is successful because he does not get into inferiority complex after that defeat. He learnt more from his defeats and tried to improve on his weakness and emerged as more powerful personality.

Inferiority complex feeling gets developed in a human being due to lack of confidence to face different situations at his work place, he lack confidence because in earlier situations he faced, he generally got dominated by others. So he has a strongly belief that others are better and knowledgeable than him, and thus has generated a complex feeling that he is less knowledgeable person.

Many people on this earth are already in grip of inferiority complex and they are having it for different things and because of that they are facing many problems.

Like some people stammer while talking, some people are not ready to interact with their bosses and some people are having lot of potential inside are not taking initiatives because they are in inferiority complex that they cannot do things.

In my school days, I was having a complex from the persons from big cities, because till Xth I was groomed in small towns, so I was having a feeling that people from city are having more exposure than me. In XIth class I moved to a big city with a feeling that they are far advanced than me and how can I compete with them. This feeling simply crush me in my first two years in city, during this period I was always having a fear that these people around me are more knowledgeable. If given a chance also I was not able to accept it because of my fear of inferiority. I developed a habit of stammering and never go to the stages to perform.

Soon when I started coming in contact with people in the city and share my ideas with them, I found that I am nowhere inferior and I started developing confidence. Soon I identified that I was feeling low without any reason, so I started taking the charge of surroundings and when I passed my XIIth exams, I was the best orator of school and the school captain.

So if we see this example also, it is very clear that sometimes our surroundings makes us to believe that we cannot perform but we have lot of potential which we hide due to feeling of inferiority. So if you just analyze your life, you can see many incidents where you were in feeling of inferiority, however at end of the day other people are less knowledgeable then you.

How to avoid this:

Whenever we are not confident on a situation and other person is more prepared and confident from us then we come in inferiority, We have to understand that in life no person is complete in all sense, everyone has one or other problem or less prepared then others and we are also part of that society only, so there is no question of inferiority, as we all are living on this earth with one or more limitations.

If any day any complex feeling comes to you and you started feeling depressed, you just remember that if you lack something, start work on that from today itself because there is never be a late beginning for a right thing.

Fear 25

A feeling which give us uncertainty and insecurity about the future, we call it fear. This feeling is also very prevalent between human beings, some people are having fear of career growth, some are of business hurdles, some are not ready to start their own business and students have fear of exams.

A very peculiar thing about fear is that till the time you face it, it is going to increase.

A candidate is having interview after a week, he is always having a fear of how it will go, how the question will be, whether I will be selected or not. This fear only goes out when he actually gives interview and finds out that there is nothing fearing. Same there is always a feeling of insecurity that comes to us when we do some important work.

Persons who are confident and have knowledge about the subject they have comparative less fearful feeling.

While taking any decision in life we should have to come out of fear otherwise it will change our perception and we can take wrong decisions i.e. we have realized that many people believe in horoscope and while starting anything they first refer to it, because they are having fear of success. If time is not suitable as per horoscope then they postpone the things for other time, which really is waste of time and money.

So we should keep this in mind that fearful feeling should not rule our mind and we should take all the decisions with rational mind.

There are always adverse effects when we come under the fearful perception and do things wrong. Why you sing a song beautifully in bathroom but when you reach at stage there is a feeling of insecurity. Why on reaching in interview room person starts stammering and forget the topic?

Fear is always a hurdle in achieving success, we always quit a work when it is near completion due to fear of failure. I.e. if you observe stock markets, it always happened like this only, whenever we leave market due to fear that prices of stock will come down, it always take a turn and started going up, so many times due to fear of losing and defeat we take some decision which finally prove to be wrong.

We generally do not invest money in a sector where there are loss made by existing companies, we simply drive conclusion that if other company is making losses we will also make losses. We do not go to our rational mind to think about the holistic picture of that particular industry.

I am quite sure, if you analyze all the loss making industry sectors while invest your money, you will find that there are nothing wrong with that particular sector, loss making is basically due to planning errors or a phase of business.

How to avoid fear

Fear can be avoided when we are firm to avoid all the fearful feelings that come to dominate our thoughts. If you analyze, every human being is born with equal capabilities, it is with time they generate all their personality, some who groom in surrounding of positive attitude, vision, confidence, decision making are less fearful and others who groom themselves in adverse surrounding are fearful.

Let's see some examples – Why some people are having fear of going in water, while some are confident of going into the water? Simple that person who know swimming are confident, so fear vanishes, if you know what to done in adverse situation then you are more well prepared. When person goes to some new city or country, he is always under the feelings of excitement and fear, how to survive, how to ask for correct destination, and what time I reached, etc. And on the other hand person who is resident of same city is very much confident in moving from one place to another because he is aware about the city, so it is clear that ignorance and lack of awareness is also a main cause of fear.

So fear in situations of life threat is inevitable like fighting with a lion etc. But those entire situations where fear is getting generated due to our own preparedness, awareness, and ignorance can be easily avoided, if we try to analyze the situation.

So explore yourself as much as possible to come out of grip of all the fears you are having because there are many fears you can overcome by exploring your own self.

Risk

26

When we are not sure of success and we are working to achieve the results, we call it as risk. In today's world risk is related with every work. So we all should be well prepared to take risk whenever required. But we should be very much sure of how to take risk because sometimes risk also place you in trouble, so while taking risk we also have to calculate it. Every decision in life required some amount of risk and we should develop an attitude of facing small and calculated risks.

Commonly, we have realized that many people in life who are working in a profession which is not of their interest, they also starts disliking their job, but they are unable to change their profession due to the factor of risk in starting fresh in their professional interest.

So if we want to define risk, we can define also, the vision and goal that we want to achieve contains certain difficulties to accomplish and there is possibility of losing also, which makes us, hindered from achieving it.

So our desire is something else but we do something else due to risk factor in between. Mostly people want to start their own business, but before starting it they give up due to the lack of confidence and high risk factor.

Advantage of Risk taking

We have to salute all those people who have taken risk in their life and made this world such a beautiful place to live.

All the inventions and growth is very good example of risk taking, if we all only do what our routine work is and do not have explore out of box because of perceived risk, then we will never achieve big results.

You might have seen many people in this world who are less educated and less knowledgeable but they have ceated immense wealth because they know how to take calculated risk.

It is a as simple as this that for making child to learn walk, we should be prepared that he will fall once or twice but he will learn how to walk, so life is also same where you may failed once or twice, but you will never be succeed till you take risk to grow.

If you want a person to learn swimming, what you have to do them, simply throw them in water they will start floating with hands and legs to swim, definitely under guidance of instructor.

For understanding risk we take example of car driver – When a person learns the car driving and is new for driving, whenever he drives car on road it is risk that he may leads to an accident, but with time when he gets experience in driving he drives comfortably. There is minimal risk when he drives because he is well prepared.

How to take risk ->

We have a very simple analysis of life, risk is a habit which you develop from your daily decisions making and handling of situation, it not something which you take all off a sudden without having any knowledge of it. If you are taking risk without having knowledge of what you may lose then it is a gamble – which I never suggest you.

All the decisions making in your professional life increase your risk taking capacity. Child starts walking then starts riding bicycle and scooter, car so on, so it is ongoing process. One successful risk give you edge to take another risk.

For having attitude to take risk, we should not be emotional and rigid person, if we are emotional then it is difficult to take risk because we are so much attached to the current surrounding that we do not want to leave it.

So if we have to rise in our life we have to take risk to make our growth fast, it may have risk of losing some money, however returns are always higher for all the calculated risks.

We have to keep in mind that risk taking is inevitable in life, if we are human beings then we have to deal with various risks today or later. So we should prepare ourselves for that now. Some things, which are risk for someone, are normal routine work for others. So it is simple that risk can also be avoided and controlled by how prepared you are to take that work.

So in professional life, why most of the assignments are been awarded to experienced people, because they are well prepared to take care of that work. If any new professional do same work it will be risk for him to do it by perfection (example of car driver).

Finally understand life to avoid risk. It is also totally situation based, some situations are risky for someone however some who are prepared for them it is not a risk.

Many people meet accidents while driving a car, many people fail as entrepreneur and many people are unable to succeed in their professional life because they are not well prepared and takes that particular profession as risk and feel fearful while doing it and finally they fail due to fear.

So risk can be completely avoided by well preparedness and positive attitude towards the problem.

Achievements

27

Every person set some goals and work accordingly to achieve those goals, if we have not set any goals also, then also routine work leads to some result, so we all have to achieve some thing or other, this is what we call as achievements.

Achievements is required in life because it is motivational and inspiring for us, these achievements also help us in positive attitude because our thoughts get processed in positive direction when we achieve anything.

Let's take an example to understand it ->

Whenever we want to make career in a certain profession, we start working towards it. On daily basis we set some goals and finally there is ultimate goal i.e. if we want to set up a factory, it requires lot of permissions, building, staff and capital, these all are our daily goals which we have to achieve and ultimate goal is that factory starts working as soon as possible with profits.

To reach at ultimate success, it is highly required to get success on all the small targets which we are facing daily, so all the small-small achievement daily makes a person motivated and dedicated towards his final goal and he achieves it.

You cannot think, that all of a sudden you become a CEO of a company. Without having all the small achievements a person cannot achieve final stage.

For winning a cricket match every player has to contribute and achieve something and contribution from all the players help us to win a match, so achievements are chain of successful work which individuals and a team has to perform to reach the final result. Contrary, on daily basis in routine life if you are unable to achieve your set targets then life can move to depression and frustration. So try to achieve as much as possible.

How to achieve

Achievements come from your dedication, commitment, vision, leadership and many more personality traits, which we have already discussed earlier.

A simple phenomenon, which works to achieve great success is to first explore all the happiness from your day-to-day achievements and this motivation which will come out from it, will take you to the great success.

If I want that next year I want promotion and you sit idle and wait for next year to get promoted, you will never get it. To get promotion you have to start working today itself on all the small targets and day to day benchmarking to achieve promotion next year easily.

This is common with every human being that we start dreaming big and forget to achieve all those small achievements, which are required to become big.

Let us take simplest example if a person is not happy in his family surroundings, how can he deliver good work and achieve better when he himself is not happy. So for every success and achievement we have to start from holistic approach of solving it.

Let me share one secret of life with all of you, may be it takes time and efforts for you to achieve your goal for the first time, but if you are able to achieve your goal you will be distinguished and can establish yourself unique then others.

Your first achievement can be big or small but it help you to build whole of your life on it because you have proved yourself that you can do it. "You can do it "is a feeling which identify a person from group of thousands peoples.

Believe me it takes lot of time for people to understand that they can achieve what they desire, it takes people whole of their life to understand what potential they are having. Thus persons should start exploring themselves as soon as they come to know that they have to achieve something they desire.

Finally achievements are ongoing process; you have to achieve things on daily basis to keep yourself happy and motivated. For successful person in life, whatever work you decide to finish or goal you set in your life, to reach at destination, then break your goal and work in small targets to achieve. And daily achieve one small target, finally you will find one day you are very near to your final target.

While travelling from Mumbai to Delhi by Train, there will be many interim stations which will continue to pass-by, every passing station you have to consider as small achievements and one step towards final target which will keep you motivated. Similarly in life you pass by small targets to reach a final target.

Ego

28

Some feeling that comes from inside and stop us interacting with others and hinder us doing work.

It is very common observation that whenever we met some of our very old friend whom we did not met from a long time, we hesitate to talk to him. This hesitation comes from the feelings that whether he or she will recognize us.

When we find our friends in a better position than us, then this hesitation grows.

Similarly for many things we hesitate talking to our boss or in event our boss has lecture us, we get angry without knowing that why he reprimand us.

Same way many people are unable to start any work & unable to make their career in the profession of their interest, for whole of their life, because their ego comes in between which hinder their thoughts to start that work.

Ego is a feeling of inferiority complex, superiority complex and sometimes feeling of fear which hinder our thoughts while we actually want to initiate any action.

Why this feeling comes to us ->

These feelings are based on situation, surrounding and are thoughts driven, which develops an attitude within ourselves that on my deed how others will react.

One of the most painful things in present world is that we always do something by positioning for other however mostly we are not aware of their actual needs.

Let's talk about success and failure, they can easily be analyzed. All the successful people generate a positive feelings or thoughts inside them for any work they do and any interaction they want perform and their ego also remain satisfied, however failures having big egos just sit in a close box and do nothing and think what others with think we cannot do anything.

We all are part of society, where we have to respect others feelings. In respecting others feelings sometimes we are so much into it, we start hurting ourselves. But still if we are hurting us we are happy because we not get any negative feedback from others and our ego gets satisfied.

Tell me one thing, is there any one out of us who is not blessed with great ideas. It comes to all of us but some people implement it and some discuss those ideas with others i.e. with friends and colleagues and if they give some negative response we feel that what we were thinking is wrong and thus we have to think in other way.

It is good to discuss your ideas with others before implementing it, but it is bad to get yourself influenced by others feelings. If we lose our confidence then next time good ideas will not come to our mind.

Disadvantage of ego

Ego always give us distance from others, due to ego we do not talk to many people and finally when they emerge as winner then we are unable to approach them because we hesitate due to ego at that time.

We are unable to start our choice of work or does not accept many jobs due to ego and finally we burn our career without starting it at all.

Additionally, If we love someone, we are unable to express our feeling because ego completely control us.

Satisfaction 29

A feeling of completeness is called satisfaction. We observe different surrounding around us, we find that everyone is busy to achieve some goals or if he has achieved something earlier, then he is occupied to achieve some another goal.

So after struggling and working also throughout our life we are not happy with our achievements in life. Every time some new desire come to our mind and we started working for it and when we achieve it then we feel satisfied for a while and start planning for something new very soon.

Why people are not satisfied.

Every human being is having many requirements and to fulfill these requirements he work throughout his life but attitude of human being is very dynamic towards life. As soon as he achieve his present requirement, he started chasing for others.

It is very good to have desire and we should always try to achieve them also. Desires help us to grow in life but here we have to keep in mind that everything which we are desiring is from our perspective, it may have some different meaning in the world, our target to achieve our desire sometimes does not have realistic targets which leads to disappointment.

One very big factor in today's' world, which is making us satisfied and unsatisfied in life is money, if you have money then you should be relatively satisfied in comparison to less wealthy because you have more options through money, however you still will have desire to earn more.

So at the end of the day, if we want to search a single satisfied man it is difficult for us.

I want to take example– Every day we take breakfast, lunch and dinner. You just analyze your state before lunch or a dinner time. If you are hungry and your desire is to have food and suppose if you get it late, you get frustrated, if you get it on time you eat it and feel satisfied, similarly next day you again want to take food to be satisfied, so it an ongoing process. If one day you did not get food at all you feel depress. Contrary if you have Just finished your lunch and someone say to you, let go to have dinner then probably you will say no because you are satisfied, however you again need it after sometime.

This is a very practical example of satisfaction – Till the time we did not achieve our goal or desire, we are after it, when we achieve our goals we feel satisfied, if we get delayed in achieving our goal we get frustrated. And after achieving goal also, we again want to achieve something else i.e. what we explain in food example that we need food every day to keep us satisfied.

So satisfaction is ongoing process, whether it is related to our work, food or any other thing, if we achieve something we will be satisfied for some time only till next desire come to our mind. And man's mind is also dynamic that new desires always comes to his mind.

Advantages of satisfaction and how to be satisfied.

When a person feel satisfied his self-esteem get boosted, satisfied person can always perform better because he is not in stage of confusions and fear. If person is satisfied he manage his work with calm and composed attitude. He does not loses his temper frequently and cope with stress better.

If you see life around you, you will find many dis satisfied people around you, some are not satisfied with job, some are not satisfied with family, with house, with car, with location, food etc.

Generally conditions do not permit us to achieve our desired things, so keep in your mind that now there is no use of pondering and generating negative thoughts about what you cannot change. It is also possible that there are some things which you can change immediately, however there are also somethings which are forever and not easily changeable, in these situations we have to explain our mind the situation instead hurting ourselves, because if you are not satisfied also, you cannot change it.

Believe me you find a rare creature on in this earth who is fully satisfied with luxury and other materialistic objects in this world. You can only make yourself happy and satisfied by asking you one question always "Is we have not tried our best to perform in all the opportunities given to us". May be there are situations and surroundings in which other people get more success than us, but one day we will get situation which will be according to us and we will be more successful than others.

So always believe in yourself and try to content your desire, after all human being is best judge for himself. You know what all are your capabilities you will find many people with same capabilities are earning more or less and persons who are earning more are not satisfied, and the person earning less is highly satisfied.

For living fully satisfied life, convince your mind everything cannot be achieved in one go, you can also achieve it when you are better prepared than others to achieve it.

So be happy and live a satisfied life. To live a satisfied life is the greatest success in this world.

Communication (Extrovert) 30

Persons who interact and talk more with others are called extrovert persons. Extrovert personality always helps us in making more friends and to know people better. If we have an extrovert personality then we ask many questions to others, which also help us in enhancing our knowledge.

In today's world extrovert personality help us in enhancing our career prospects like in sales, marketing, customer care and other fields, where interaction with customer is required. Generally it is observed that extrovert persons are good communicators.

Today's work require good communications, which is always easier for an extrovert person than introvert.

So if primarily we see direct communication, we find two types of person's extroverts and introverts.

Introverts peoples are less interactive and less talkative but they are good listeners. Extrovert always enjoy a company of introvert person and vice-versa because both are compatible.

Good communication is one very good tool in corporate world and business environment. If we talk about our communication again we can divide it in two forms – one is business communication and other is personal communication.

Business communication should be precise to the point and emphasis should be on the subject. To be a winner in business you should have to be good in written as well in oral communication.

In personal communication it will be something, where people feel delight talking to you.

Communication is important because it is only the route between you and other person for creating relationship. If you know this route you can cultivate relationship easily.

Let's take few examples to understand communication.

You must have analyzed in your life that you always feel happy and secure, talking to a person who gives you and your thoughts respect i.e. you must always prefer going to shop keeper who talks with you politely and understand your requirement, rather than going to a shopkeeper who is arrogant in spite you find more things there.

So first lesson in communication is to respect other thoughts and get respect for our thoughts.

Second lesson - As good you are in communication, same you have to be good in identifying others requirement.

An arrogance never work, try to be humble all the time.

How to develop communication skills

Communication skill are developed from our overall personality and communication also help us in developing personality.

It is an ongoing process where we develop these skills from surroundings and different situations. Communication skills starts developing from child hood only, we first get different chances to develop it in our family and then we get it to develop in school by various ways like reading, writing and interacting others. In college we start doing group discussions to develop our communication skills and in our working also, we daily going on enhancing it by meeting with different people. So these all are some common platforms, where we all get chance to develop communication skills, still some are having good communication skill than others, it is because communication skills are your reflection of personality, communication skill shapes itself in the way your personality is, that is why it is different from people to people. Persons who take initiatives and leadership qualities they are having different communication than person who is fearful.

So to generate a powerful communication skills, you first have to generate personality traits these personality traits will get reflected in communication.

We have to keep in our mind that whenever we have to start anything in our life whether it pertains to business or personal, first thing which other notices is your communication – If you fail in your first appearance then you will not going to get further chances. So we should be ready with excellent communication skills.

Whenever we are in an interview or we are writing an important letter or we are discussing some important business issues with our financier, we have to be very much sure that we have to perform with our best skills. We have to keep in mind, if we do not give best we will be the only loser and only thing which differentiate from a winner with loser is confidence. So be confident and present your best communication skills. Confidence only comes from our skills. Why we give good speech and sing good songs when we are talking to someone junior to us or in our friends, because we are sure of that what we are doing is correct and others will get impress out of it. And there is no fear of losing anything, our communication skills gets hindered when there is fear of losing some thing, which, generally happens when we are talking on important issue.

Communication skills is also within our own self only, you might have observed some people who stammer while talking, this is because they have undergone certain situations and surrounding from where they have lost their confidence and they have feeling of insecurity that they are unable to speak words. But these all are our mental blocks only that we cannot speak words. These persons when talk to themselves in alone they never stammer they talk perfectly. So how it is possible that we can perform a thing alone but are unable to perform in front of people. This is nothing else but lack of confidence. Stage fear is very common, but when people stammer with their friends also means they are taking every platform as public stage only and they become conscious about their speaking. Where you are doubtful about your capabilities and you become alert and whenever we are alerted, we do not behave in normal way. Whenever we are not normal be pretend and when we pretend we also lost our original competences. So for better and effective communication you should be natural.

One major thing, which we always have to keep in mind for good communication is never think that "what others will think about us" this is, only fear which hides our communication. I have told this earlier also no one is bothered about what we are speaking or doing because everyone is having one or other limitations.

Career

31

Every person on earth has to choose some work area where he has to perform to build his career. So career is the work area where we want to work and through that we achieve what we want.

Career is something, which should be planned well in advance in life so that we can start as early as possible to achieve it.

Some people always remain confused while setting careers about which career to choose in life. This thing is found most commonly in students – but the most simple answer for this is, career should be in area of your interest, because every field give us wonderful opportunities, it is we only who has to explore the potential of that field.

Some people due to some constraints and limitations unable to choose their interest as their field, so in these situations they should have to generate or involve themselves in their work, so that interest can be created, because without interest you cannot do justice with your job and with justice you can achieve your career goals.

I saw many people biased about some career options and thinking other options to be not worthwhile, practically which is not true, i.e. in India people generally choose from two career options i.e. engineer and doctor. If they are unable to be successful in these options then they go for others, but can anyone of you tell me are engineers and doctors are only successful persons on this earth? "NO". There are many more persons who are successful by deciding their career goal as per their interest.

You must also have observed that there are hundreds of areas where people are working and making this world a better place to live.

Why I am pushing on your interest as your career option because anything, which is new and unique in this world, has more value.

This is also true that, when economy grows, it create many work areas to work with. If we talk in present scenarios engineers, doctors etc. are much suited areas, but you can really come up something which is other then this, just go for it, it will be more rewarding.

For reaching the career of your choice vision, dedication and decision-making plays big roles. Initially if we see that struggle is part of every new career or career which we want to achieve, so no short cuts are allowed in career making, i.e. If we think that we will choose a career where we can achieve more without struggling less then answer is "no". For reaching to career goals every person has to work hard, it is immaterial at what period of life he has given time to achieve that career. If at all some people achieve success fast are due to their personality development.

One more thing we have to keep in mind is that no career is good or bad. Likewise people compare with cricket player or an actor having a very good career, true these people are having glamour and they earn more money in small period but career is of limited time, but other careers are long lasting and always rewarding. If we take an example of small shopkeeper, he also earns money for whole of his life, once his shop gets set and renowned.

Finally while choosing career we should be very careful about all the outcome, growth and potential of that career. If it is your interest also it is good, because once you are in it, it is not easy to come out. While working on your career path do not get hindered by all the troubles which comes your way because they are the milestones which you have to cross for finally reaching your destination.

Versatile 32

Person having knowledge of most of surroundings and situations is called versatility.

Versatility is developed in a person from his approach of learning. It is very easy to develop versatility within our self. For developing it we have to do nothing extra.

Daily we face many situations, with different surroundings and we interact with many people of different nature, so different things are always going around us, we simply have to widen our scope and look things from a holistic approach to get versatility. For example we all have observed scenarios where sometimes power shut off from our houses and offices and we immediately call an electrician to see what is the fault, and when he come he just replace the fuse wire and things again starts working. We did not know what he has done because at that time we were busy in talking to some of the irrelevant issues because we got break from work for some time. If we see once what he has done, then may be if another time same thing happened, we not even have to call him and we can do it on our own. So like this many things goes on around us, we simply have to see what all are happening because we get enough time to observe their rectification process also but we ignore thinking what's the use. So we have to develop attitude within ourselves, where we always have to try to learn all the things that we find good for our future.

Versatile people are acceptable at most of the places because of their understanding and compatibility goes high with the environment. These people's perception gets changed because they are more aware of the surroundings.

We all are having two hands but very few people do work with same efficiency from both the hands. Everyone uses one hand only to do all the works. So for our self also we are do not use both hands and leave one hand unutilized, then what to talk about external things. In other way, best use of resources from our creative attitude is also called versatile nature.

So externally and internally, we leave many things unused in our life, which can really change our fortune, if we use them, this is what we call as versatile nature.

With every new thing which you know extra than your normal routine work always motivate yourself and generate lot of confidence.

In today's life we have to interact with many people in personal life and business life. It may be party, meetings and general discussion and in all these places we all have observed that, there are some other topics also except subject(which we are mainly discussing)come, because in between we get time, here the versatile person take edge of the group and dominates.

In actual life it is true, that only those people survive who are fit as per the surroundings, survival of the fittest is nothing else than your adjustment capabilities as per requirements. Only those person can adjust themselves who are have versatile nature.

Punctual 33

Strictly following the time schedule as per the requirement of situations and surroundings.

Punctuality in life helps us in, to take our life in a right direction. It is a discipline, which starts from small time management, but its impact on the life is immense.

Most of the time we reach late at different places, something it is in our conscious mind, why to reach early, lets other also come and then we reach. Two things which get impacted with this are that you make a habit of generally delaying your decisions which will impact your over all personality.

Officially, if strictly you people maintain discipline of punctuality it will you one great advantage of always available on time and today it is very required that you should be approachable when it is required.

How punctuality come

How it is possible that we always reach 5 minutes before our train arrival time, because we know that if we are late then train will not wait for us, it will leave, so our internal mind programmed accordingly.

But in other case where it is not very strict schedule, we did not take time schedule strictly, however if we try then we can easily reach on time also.

Now think of a situation where train comes late and you are waiting since 1 hour, how disappointing it feels, so by not adhering with time schedule others also get affected similarly. When you do not reach on time, it is a definite loss for you but may be you also have wasted others time who are waiting for you.

Punctual behavior is outcome of your disciplined approach. It is we only who take things as granted or due to our laziness we do not adhere to time schedule. I don't know why we waste our time in trivial things, when we have some important meeting with someone.

Advantages

Sometimes we feel that reaching on time will not going to yield us anything, but it is not true, it is a habit and it only get generated from our day to day routine work. If you are punctual in all your work your internal self will not allow you to delay any work. Punctual behavior is liked by everyone, it is not like that that we have to ponder on what time we have to reach, etc.

Punctuality starts from time management and move to every area of your work. You are able to perform your office responsibilities well on time. Delay is like a wide spread disease, if you start making it, it will grip you and your all the work will be pending. If you try also then you will not come out it and get lag behind in your profession. So adhere yourself on time with whichever field of life it is.

Respect 34

When we consider others thoughts and feeling means we are giving them respect. Respect is to make other feels that you are not ignoring him and care for them.

Respect has got different advantages, if you respect someone you always get respect back. Others always love you, people will not feel insecure in your presence and people will try to come close to you.

Every person has some ego and need to be respected in dealings. You can fulfill both there requirements and give people self-esteem.

When you observe in your surroundings, you will find many people who are liked by others and people prefer their company in parties and other places. The reason is very simple, they feel that they will going to get good behavior and respect from them.

Now just analyze some crucial situations in your life, when you are working on some important assignment and you have to interact with many people to get it done, i.e. your surrounding are having juniors and seniors i.e. every type of people. In this particular situation you must be delighted by all those people who all have given you proper response however you must have felt frustrated with those who have ignored you during this assignment.

We are sometimes unaware of the power of respecting others, respecting others will get for you much more respect in return and will change your life. Respect is totally based on giving and taking relations, you have to give respect to take respect from others.

In life we come across many situations where we have to respond to someone on some work or some requirement. We can always respond in two ways, one way is to give proper answer to others and second to ignore them, which might hurt others.

So while saying no to someone also, we can put in a nice way, which will not hurt a person.

Believe me it happens if you see your past, you will find that there are many people whom you respect because of their good attitude towards others.

While we respect others it will cost nothing to us but other person will think jubilant. So we should always keep in mind that while interacting with someone, we should take care that they will not get hurt unnecessarily with our talk and deeds, because we will get more from them if we respect others, if we ignore others, will get nothing out of it which is of no use.

How to respect

It is always a big question to every one of us that what behavior of us will makes other person happy. In general life we have observed that all the people whom we interact sooner or later, we come to know what they like and what they do not like, what behavior they expect from others, we simply have to be careful in all the interaction which we make with them and always react in way which they like. If we see whole of our life and analyze it, we can come out with this conclusion only, that all the persons whom we annoyed or make angry, we could also have avoid that by simply dealing carefully with them because it is always in back of our mind that what type of behavior is accepted by others. While interacting for the first time, we should always be very humble because our softness in approach is always considered as language of a good man.

Don't confuse respect with fear. Respect is the way of our behavior where we try to give other person reflexes and feeling what is expected from us and what others deserves. It will never allow others to make a perception that we are a weak personality.

If you respect others, then others will really going to help you due to the respect which you have given them.

Rewards 35

Any appreciation, which we receive for our work done, or any success, we call as reward. Reward is very good motivation factor where we feel honored and other identifies us.

Rewards are such milestones in life, which keeps life moving, if we get them on regular interval of time. Can anyone imagine a success, which is not recognize by anyone neither any reward has been received for that?

Generally when we work hard and reach towards the goal, we want that goal should reach us in form of reward only, if we are unable to achieve it, then we get shattered. So reward and appreciation is something, which should come time to time in our life so that we feel happy, motivated and inclined towards progress.

How to achieve Award :- So this is quite sure that, everyone want to be rewarded in life, but getting reward means we have to do something which is better than our surrounding or unique.

So when we start working for some appreciation and reward, we should have to be sure in self that we will do it. This confidence will leads us to success. This confidence is to be developed on our own, rarely surrounding gives this confidence.

So first, reward is always from your current surroundings, when you prove yourself there, Once you tasted success in your current surrounding then a passion with motivation comes to you within yourself, which will lead you for further success. To reach at highest point, step one by one, because to reach at top we have to receive lot many appreciation in between to get motivated and move further. If we are unable to get in between appreciation, then sometimes depression and other negative feelings surround us, which hinders our growth.

Let's take example to understand this phenomenon:-

Students gradually go from one standard to second till XIIth and college and further to professional study. So at every level you are getting appreciation and rewarded to move towards success.

Generally in different life situation, it is similar, where we should gradually increase by taking all the appreciation desired.

So if any discipline or path, we are defining for our self, then we should be aware of this fundamental of life that we require motivation from time to time otherwise we feel depressed.

For receiving appreciation we can also make such friends which are really good motivators because some times without any reason if our friends start finding fault in us then, we reach at a stage of fear and distrust.

Finally reward is a non-ending process in life, where for every achievement you get this. So be ready to work accordingly because with every reward what so ever you get, you started planning the next, to achieve bigger milestone. So life is a cycle which moves like this.

Like farmer who sow seeds and wait for his crops for some months but every passing day comes as rewards to him when he see his crop growing daily and this factor give him passion, delight and motivation till he reaches to the final stage. Same in life you get different surprises, which make your life good for living.

Knowledge

36

To know about surroundings is knowledge, as we have discussed earlier also we face many situations daily with different surroundings, if we have knowledge of surroundings in those situations, then it can be resolved easily and give our personality a good perspective.

Knowledge plays a main differentiator in successful and unsuccessful person because without having knowledge you cannot effectively solve the problems.

To be successful manger or leader, knowledge is the key word.

Remember any meeting or gathering where you have participated and how swiftly someone took the charge of the meeting and emerge as a leader in that group because he has suggested something which is liked by others. This suggestion is something, which is comes out of knowledge only. It may be that the person is having a good communication skill, that is why he took the charge, but communication skills also get enhanced, if you have good knowledge about the subject.

Human beings are having a peculiar quality of adjusting their personality as per situations. For adjustment of your personality you require knowledge about the particular thing because you cannot be confident and expressive till you know about the subject. So any change in life or new situation of life, a knowledgeable person can handle it better due to the confidence he has due to his knowledge.

In this competitive world everyone is equipped with lot of knowledge inside him, but still some people always lead and some follow due to the level of knowledge both possess. So you should be having knowledge as much as you can because it is a never-ending process, more you learn you will get more.

Firstly knowledge comes from our school, family and college, which we call as basic education. This is generally common about every one, and then we learn many things from our offices and day-to-day working. We people face many situations, which are difficult, but we resolve them. The learning, which we get by solving day to day problems are real knowledge, this broadens our horizon, confidence and leadership qualities. Because most of the situations are common in the world, if we have already faced it once, then we can better help others to get rescue out of it.

To have a drastic improvement in your working, I want to suggest you an approach of work it is very simple but do not know how many of us follow this.

Before entering or starting any work try to gain information as much as possible about work that will really help you in understanding and doing it faster with less efforts.

Simple work also gets difficult and we do it wrong, if we are not having knowledge about that. For example – Generally it happens in our life that we have to locate address of some of our friend. While taking address, we both forget to exchange some landmark near the house which will help us to locate friend's house much easily, so we waste lot of time in locating house of our friend which is side by a sweet shop which is very famous.

So knowledge consists of our vision, attitude, awareness and dedication towards work.

Knowledge is required in whatever field you are, it is not as such that you survive in a profession without any knowledge. So again, I want to suggest you to get yourself one hour in a day, where you can think on your progress, growth and if any failure in life, you will automatically come with solution or you will find the ways where you have to increase knowledge to get yourself successful.

Frustration 37

On non-achievement of works related to our official or personal life causes feeling of frustration. Frustration is again a very bad personality trait, which always keep on disturbing us till we achieve that particular goal. But generally if we get frustrated, then it is more prominent that we will not be able to reach at the height we want, because our thoughts which control our action changes to negative territory. Following we turn negative, we start cursing our self and our attitude towards life changes. We lose confidence and move to depression.

Frustration feeling always grips us when we are aiming at work something which is beyond our capabilities and we still want to achieve it. In this case it take years to develop ourselves till that level and we assume from our failures that we are unable to achieve it due to our inability.

So, the most common frustration type is mentioned above where our desire is always to achieve the things as early as possible, but to reach to our goals, we should have to be actually prepared, so why to give our self-such a painful treatment where our thought always give us bad feelings and we feel very uncomfortable and unhappy which in turns generate lot of stress and illness.

So frustration can be avoided if we understand our requirement and capabilities and time them accordingly.

Generally you all must have observed that in office places we always think why we are not on next senior position instead having more capabilities or why we are not promoted when we have performed. There are many more questions like this, which always comes to our mind and get us frustrated and depressed. Such feelings which inspire us, we should always take them as motivational factor that still we are in race.

In Athletics most common event is 100m race, which gives whole world the fastest man on this earth. Every year or two there is someone who clocked best time and win the race. All the competitions are having world records like 100 m race. So we have to understand this fact of life that efforts and knowledge are not controlled by anybody, if there is someone on this earth who is more dedicated to achieve the same goal, he will achieve it, so there should be no place for frustration. Frustration also comes when we are unable to perform as per our capabilities. Again if you are unable to perform that particular work as per your capabilities because of other factors, which are not controlled by you then you should not have to feel frustrated. So always try to take inspiration from the all the failure, as frustration will take you to dark end and learning from the incidence will open way for a bright future.

How to avoid Frustration

Frustration generally comes from the attitude of comparisons and jealousy, which we have already discussed in length in earlier chapters, but here also, I want to give you a simple trick to avoid it. Everyone who are having frustrating feeling due to any reason has to analyze themselves for a while and think of millions of people who are less privileged then you. So this is a live path where we all have to grow and while fulfilling our ambition we face challenges, where it may happen that we fail, so we have to take them as opportunity to learn from them and come out of frustration feeling because they are of no use at all.

Polite 38

While communicating you should be careful that others should not get hurt, whether it oral, written, body language or any type of communication. It should be done by keeping other person perspective also in mind, so politeness is a tool in your communication, which can make you, win over others which others expect.

In this world we meet hundreds of people daily and they all have different expectations from us, it is also not possible for human being to satisfy all the expectations of other because we practically don't know what he wants. But one thing, which is always in our hand, is our behavior and this we can control by politeness. By our politeness we can dig a person within and come out with other requirements, which in many cases makes person successful.

If you are in customer oriented business you know how important it is to know what others expect from us, on others expectation only we have to build our self to win them.

Let's understand it much better, can we make a building if foundation is not there? Same politeness is foundation, which always give you a place where you can stand firmly and built there on.

If you look back in your life and you analyze your life, you yourself would find that you prefer going to person who are polite in giving response to different problems. So same with us, people will really be delighted to come close to us if they know they will not be hurt.

People always prefer going to a grassland with lot of flowers than to go to a thorny plants in jungle.

So our politeness always give us a great space to build there on future behavior with other person.

By politeness it is not that you have to talk sweet only and the feelings of others are crucified, "no". Politeness means to provide complete delight to others by taking others perspective.

In general we have seen we are polite with powerful persons and elders more than our counter parts and juniors. I believe all require same treatment of love and affection by your polite behavior.

Politeness is an art, which over all reflect from your language, words and body language, so it is not like that you want to show to be polite with others then you can show it. It will be there, but perfection will come when you really try it.

I do not want to convey that you be polite and give others happiness and when it is turn of others they only gives you rude and unexpected type of behavior. Here you can change behavior accordingly. My main concern is that we have to control on ourselves and our behavior should always start from politeness only if sometimes situation is not ready to except politeness from other that we should have to act accordingly, but in very rare situations.

Why this is been observed that when people raise to big positions in life they become more polite, means politeness is totally reacted with how satisfied you are in life, so why we want to prove others, that we are not satisfied in life by communicating in a manner which will going to neither help us nor to others.

To be polite and for good communication, we should be keep in mind that we have to react in same way what we expect from others, then all the time we find our behavior traits make us others happy.

Politeness also helps us in keeping our self-calm and composed so that our stress level is always in controlled.

One simple fact of life that aggressive behaviors takes more energy and are not as effective as politeness, so by utilizing less energy we are able to get more results, so why to opt for anything else.

So we have to understand this that politeness is always a sign of respect, contentment and peace, where by saying nothing about yourself, you declare yourself to be happy and satisfied and others take it same way.

How can you make others happy and convince on your point when you are not happy and matured.

So practice politeness, as it will yield always better results.

Sorry/Understanding our mistakes 39

Accepting your mistake is sorry. Sorry used at appropriate time is very helpful however frequent use of sorry also loses it worth.

It is very good and understandable that if we all start realizing where we are wrong and correct it.

The biggest problem in human behavior is sometimes that they go so much adamant that they are not ready to accept what they are doing may be wrong also. It is good you are confident and firm about your decision that you are right and that is why you are adamant, but maybe our perception at that point of view is wrong.

This is very common behavior traits where people are not ready to understand what is the perfect solution for the situation, and everyone impose their own decision and things comes to a dead lock. Here comes the attitude of accepting, we can all amicably sit and can come out with a solution. Here may be ideas of some people are accepted some are not but only the right perspective will be taken care off.

This is explained very well in the example by the elephant given in perception chapter. So many times in our life it happens like this that situation and surrounding changes our perceptions and we are not able to have the true picture and we start thinking from different angle and make others also unhappy.

Let try to understand it from a simple example – if we are returning from a horror movie in night and we are walking by a road, which is dark and we all of a sudden see snake is moving side by us, due to that we start shouting however actually it was a rope.

Try to understand our life also, in this way the type of feeling which comes to our mind, drive the thoughts and sometimes leads to wrong perception and we become adamant that we are correct and make others unhappy, which is a very common phenomenon in life.

Daily at our work place we have to take many decisions, for taking decision different persons emerges with different ideas due to different perception, it does not mean that they are wrong, it means they have perceived problem from different angle and may be they have better solution.

Generally all the mistakes which we make are due to different perception, what we are having. We are still doing what we know, so if any day we come to know that we are on wrong approach, so there is nothing bad in passing sorry, if we have hurt others or we have to accept within self.

Saying sorry can easily solve so all the thing, which unintentionally we start doing wrong due to perception mistakes.

By saying sorry it reflects you are quite adjustable person and others also feel happy that you are at least ready to listen to them.

In India long back when bus services just got started and the first time when a bus went to a village and when villagers saw it for the first time they offer grass in front of the bus to eat. So it is perception only where you understand bus as an animal.

Printed in the United States
By Bookmasters